D1433061

HERBERT SPENCER

HERBERT SPENCER

BY

HUGH SAMUEL ROGER ELLIOT

 BOOKS FOR LIBRARIES PRESS
FREEPORT, NEW YORK

First Published 1917 as part of
Makers of the Nineteenth Century Series
Reprinted 1970

STANDARD BOOK NUMBER:
8369-5203-0

LIBRARY OF CONGRESS CATALOG CARD NUMBER:
75-107800

PRINTED IN THE UNITED STATES OF AMERICA

GENERAL EDITOR'S PREFACE

WHATEVER may be thought to-day of the value of Spencer's writings, no one who wishes to understand the thought of the nineteenth century can neglect him. His system of philosophy influenced his generation, not only in England, but in America and elsewhere; even those most profoundly antagonistic to it thought it necessary to reckon with it and answer it : in science, though not entirely in accord with Darwin, he helped to popularise evolutionary ideas : in politics he represented, if he did not lead, a body of opinion which had great influence in his day, an influence which even in these warlike times, so abhorrent as they would have been to Spencer, is not entirely dead. Mr. Elliot's qualifications for the task of expounding Herbert Spencer's already almost neglected tenets to the present generation are well brought out in his introductory chapter. Once a fervent admirer of Spencer, so fervent that he carried volumes of the philosopher about with him when campaigning in the South African veldt, he has since re-read him, and without losing all his former love can criticise Spencer in the light of history and of to-day's needs. As far as one can see, whether as a philosopher or a man of science, Spencer is not likely to live for future generations. If he lives at all, it will no doubt be as a political thinker, representative of a school of politicians, wedded to individualism and to peace, who, though never hitherto able to resist the torrent of national excitement at its height, are likely always to persist as they have in our past history, not least when we have been engaged in great wars which have held the imagination of the majority; the school represented by a Bedford in Chatham's day, a Fox or a Stanhope in the day of Chatham's son, a Cobden and a Bright in the Victorian era.

BASIL WILLIAMS.

CHELSEA,
  September, 1916.

PREFACE

I HAVE pleasure in making acknowledgments of assistance (mostly unconscious) rendered me in the preparation of this volume by many of Herbert Spencer's friends. My estimate of his character is based, not only on a careful study of all his published works, and of works written about him by others, but on conversations carried on, many of them years ago, with such friends of Spencer as Lord and Lady Courtney, Mrs. Sidney Webb, Mrs. Henry Hobhouse, the late Mrs. Meinertzhagen, Mr. Henry Tedder, Sir Ray Lankester, the late Dr. Charlton Bastian, Mr. Geoffrey Williams (Spencer's publisher), the late Mr. Thomas Mackay, and others. The view I have presented of Spencer, however, is my own.

I have to thank the Herbert Spencer Trustees for permission to publish a letter ; and also Mr. Geoffrey Williams for showing me the letter ; and more particularly for lending me a copy of the original and private edition of the Autobiography, of which six copies only were printed in all. I have to thank him further for the loan of a copy of the suppressed book " The Nature and Reality of Religion," which is now altogether unobtainable.

H. E.

CONTENTS

HERBERT SPENCER

CHAPTER I

INTRODUCTION

THE relation of philosophy to war is a question
that has occupied many of the most powerful
minds in all countries through all ages. The study
of that question has lately received a new impetus
on account of the terrible events now in progress
throughout the continent of Europe. Wide interest
has been centred upon the works of those German
thinkers who represent, and who are partially
responsible for, that morbid state of mind which
seeks gratification in wars of conquest and the
military organisation of society. Nietzsche, Bernhardi, and Treitschke have been constantly cited
as typical of the degrading militarism of modern
Germany. It is perhaps true that the first-named
of these writers has been somewhat unjustly
accused, and that we should regard Fichte and
Hegel rather than Nietzsche as the true philosophic apostles of German militarism. However
this may be, it is clear that many of the leading
German philosophers have regarded militarism
with a friendly eye.

People in general scarcely realise how different
has been the outlook of English philosophers.
It is natural that the country most abandoned to
the ideals of militarism should have produced
the philosophers most sympathetic to those ideals.
We in this country sometimes forget that we have
in the past been the least military (though, as
Moltke said, perhaps the most warlike) of all
the nations of Europe. And many are scarcely
aware that the main philosophic attacks upon
the doctrines of militarism have come from English
thinkers, and reached their climax last century
in the writings of Herbert Spencer. If we have
studied the works of those German authors who
are said to have brought on the present conflagra-
tion, we ought surely to study also the works of
our own philosopher, who long ago foresaw the
goal of European policy, and contended with all
his might to stem the tide before it was too late.

For undoubtedly the main interest of Spencer's
works at present is on the social side. His scientific and evolutionary writings have already
become part of the " atmosphere " of modern
thought, in the sense that they scarcely need to be
taught, but constitute the foundation upon which
more recent ideas are built. But his social writings
have not in the same way become axiomatic. On
the contrary, the political tendencies before the
war were all hostile to Spencer's teaching. It

appears highly probable that, after the war, political currents will again run in favour of Spencerian ethics, if for no other reason because State-economy will be the order of the day, and State-economy is at the root of Spencer's social philosophy. At all events, it seems to be clear that the social policy against which Spencer fought is now bankrupt. It has failed, and its failure threatens to ruin Europe for a generation. It does not follow, indeed, that Spencer's dogmatic individualism will henceforth be triumphantly established : that can never be. But it does follow that certain important truths or principles, which he emphasised, will when shorn of their dogmatism occupy a far larger part of the field of attention than heretofore.

Spencer's position in philosophy is a comparatively isolated one. He received little from the writings of previous philosophers, but much from the science of his own time. Nevertheless his philosophic affinities were with the naturalistic, and even the materialistic, thinkers of the past, rather than with the idealists or the metaphysicians. Let it not be supposed that I use the word " materialism " in its degraded popular signification. I use it only in illustration of that tendency towards hard facts and practical common sense which has been so eminently characteristic of Scottish and English philosophers in the past. In his purely scientific writings, as in his social writings, Spencer was peculiarly an English philosopher. He could not read German : he loathed German philosophers ; and such part of his controversial writings as were not devoted to the condemnation of the Prussian type of militarism and socialism were occupied largely with attacks upon German metaphysics. Of all great thinkers, he owed less to German influence than any other who can be named. His philosophy was wholly English by spirit and descent, save perhaps for some resemblances to the Scottish school of Realism. His social philo-sophy, pivoting on liberty and the limitations of State-duties, is so pre-eminently English that it is impossible to imagine the production of such a work in any other race of people. Seeing that we are already well acquainted with the writings of Treitschke and Bernhardi, with the aims and spirit of the German people, may we not now with advantage turn to study the philosopher who, more than any other, expresses our own spirit, and sums up the aims and character of the free citizen of Britain ? Let us visualise clearly not only the principles, *against* which we are fighting, but those *for* which the British Empire has always stood in the past.

I do not mean that we are all likely to agree with Spencer : far from it. It is not the overt doctrines, but the spirit underlying them, with which we are in sympathy. And since we are compelled, for

the destruction of militarism, to assume temporarily a military organisation ourselves, it behoves
us now particularly to keep our minds fixed upon
the great ideal of liberty, which we hope to establish more firmly than ever upon the conclusion
of peace.

In attempting to place before my readers a
judicial estimate of the true value of Spencer's
philosophy, I may perhaps be pardoned if I
describe my own relation towards it. It has been
my singular fortune (or fate) to have read through
the whole of Spencer's works twice at an interval
of fifteen years, and each time in the midst of a
great war. The first reading in fact was carried
out on active service on the South African veldt,
where not infrequently I had little other baggage
than a toothbrush and a volume of " The Principles of Psychology." There exists in the English
language no more trenchant indictment of war
and militarism than is contained in " The Study
of Sociology." Yet it was my lot to read that
work many miles from any inhabited town, in
momentary expectation of an attack, and with
revolver ready loaded in case of sudden need.
To a certain type of mind, Spencer's doctrine of
social freedom is irresistibly attractive : even more
so than his easy naturalistic interpretation of
phenomena, expressed as it is in a style of extreme
lucidity. Spencer appeals so much to the

sentiments that his writings tend to excite either
hostility or dogmatic discipleship. The latter was
my case, and it was only after years of watching
English politics that the discipleship tended to
apathy : for the realisation of Spencer's theories
appeared to be hopeless.

But the outbreak of a new and far more terrible
war has already done much to break up the
political agnosticism which had settled over a
large section of the British people. We are once
again in the presence of real issues. We are no
longer drifting slowly along the placid stream of
social reform, increasing month by month our
stock of legislative enactments, and adding year
by year to the powers of the Government over
the individual. Circumstances have driven us
headlong to a consummation which in many spheres
touches the limit to which previous legislation
was gradually progressing. In a few months the
power of the State has increased to a degree which
it could scarcely have attained in as many years
of social reform. If the State formerly was by
degrees asserting its authority over individuals, if
it was always enlarging its claim to control their
activities and to take their incomes as taxation ;
it has now overtly proclaimed its complete
authority over the persons and the incomes of
every individual subject to its control. Doubtless
it has done so by necessity ; but here we have a

definite and avowed social policy, which is exceedingly likely to be continued long after the temporary necessity has lapsed. Is this a satisfactory
social policy, or is it not ? That is the question
which Spencer's philosophy endeavours to decide.
On the one hand there is the argument that the
State, advised by the most highly trained experts,
is better able to decide what men ought to do
than the average semi-educated citizen can decide
it for himself. There is then the second step—
namely, after seeing what is right for men to do,
there arises the question as to whether they should
all be compelled to do it. In most of the legislation
in vogue before the war these doctrines were
tacitly implied, and they were scarcely at all
resisted. They are now overtly proclaimed ; and
as soon as the necessity of the moment has passed
we shall have before us the question of their real
validity.

On the other hand there is simply the doctrine
of freedom, and all the mental qualities which freedom implies. It is that doctrine which Spencer's
philosophy endeavours to establish ; it will be
examined later in the light of his philosophy
and of subsequent events. At present we are
much more citizens than men, and much more
subjects than citizens. Probably most people will
decide the question forthwith by reference to their
personal sentiments ; but it is a question which

at all events is of first importance. We are at
length in the presence of a real issue, to be solved,
if possible, in the light of reason and inquiry, and
without prejudice.

Once again, during the progress of a war, have
I read Spencer's furious declamations against
warlike and military activities. But now in many
parts I find the arguments ill-founded ; in other
parts the conclusions are certainly false ; and the
style which formerly appeared so lucid now seems
to have settled down to a deadly and invariable
monotony. Yet still the thought arises, that,
if Europe had followed Spencer, this war could
never have occurred. Europe is now drenched
in blood ; its wealth and prosperity are fast being
drained away. The spirit of Treitschke has
triumphed over the spirit of Spencer—the metaphysics of Germany over the common sense of
England. And while reading Spencer again, I
have reached the conviction that, notwithstanding
his errors, his spirit was sound and true. It is
useless now to sneer at liberty as a discredited
doctrine. Europe may have abandoned it ; but
see the result ! The social philosophy which can
take effect like this is unquestionably and irremedi-
ably false. It does not follow, however, that the
rival system is wholly true. We must certainly
discard the whole dogmatism and formulary of
Spencer's social philosophy : we cannot force the

conclusions of sociology into a few narrow and rigid laws, as Spencer endeavoured to do. The *data* are so complicated that we can only see the issues " as through a glass darkly." We can discuss only the vague outlines of a few very general truths : we cannot see the sharp and detailed outlines that most politicians imagine, or that certain philosophers labour to describe.

Those who have had to deal with biography soon become aware that, whereas the lives of men of action are full of interest and detail, the lives of men of thought are barren of incident : for they live in their writings and not in their doings. The chronicler of Spencer's doings has little to tell. His life was *par excellence* in his writings ; and a true biography of Spencer must consist chiefly of an account of his works. He was one of those authors of whom it may be most truly said that his works were much greater than himself; and all the best of him will be found in his philosophy. His personality, outside his works, was meagre and petty. In this biography, therefore, I shall devote the greater part of the space to an account of his writings, in which he sacrificed the greater part of his personality.

CHAPTER II

HERBERT SPENCER was born in Derby on April 27, 1820. He came from a family chiefly noticeable for their strong individuality and dissenting tendencies. His grandfather, Matthew Spencer, who was born in 1762, settled in Derby early in life as assistant in St. Peter's parish school. About 1791 he became head of a school himself, where he taught, according to one of his advertisements, "reading, writing, merchants' accounts, mensuration (with land surveying), algebra, etc." For board and education, his terms were thirteen guineas a year, with an entrance fee of one guinea. Matthew Spencer had six sons, of whom the eldest, William George Spencer, was the father of the philosopher. He was commonly called George Spencer, and was thus distinguished from a younger brother who had also received the name of William. George Spencer assisted his father in the management of the school and inherited from him at his death the property of the family, consisting of a few cottages and two fields. He married in 1819 the daughter of a plumber and glazier, called Harriet Holmes, who, notwithstanding a "small infusion of Huguenot blood and trace of Hussite blood," was a woman of very ordinary character, showing little of the rebellious tendencies of the Spencer family. She is described as patient and gentle— qualities altogether opposite to those of her husband; and the divergence of interests and character did not conduce to a happy married life. George Spencer followed the career of teacher throughout his life; he was brought up as a Wesleyan, but in later years turned more naturally towards the sect of the Quakers. He exhibited much of the unbending discipline of that doctrine : he would never address his correspondents as "Esquire" or "Reverend," but always as "Mr."; nor would he ever take off his hat to anyone, of whatever rank. He was keenly interested in abstract questions of science and politics; was honorary secretary of the Derby Philosophical Society, and by politics a Whig with tendencies towards what would later have been called Philosophic Radicalism. A man of aggressive independence and much ability and originality, he became somewhat irritable in later years, especially with his wife, whose questions and observations he used often wholly to ignore. He had nine children in all, but only Herbert, the eldest, passed the stage of infancy; his four brothers and four sisters all died in early years. It is often said that great men tend to derive their characters from their mothers; but the case of Herbert Spencer certainly runs counter to the generalisation, for he had many and striking mental resemblances to his father, and none whatever discernible to his mother.

His education was of course very unusual, and was mainly characterised by lack of coercion. It was as widely different as possible from that of John Stuart Mill, who began to learn Greek when he was three, and who was intensively cultivated to an almost incredible degree. Spencer, on the contrary, was left largely to himself: he was very backward as a boy in the ordinary subjects of children's lessons, but he had derived from observation of Nature, etc., a considerable amount of miscellaneous information. At the age of thirteen he knew "nothing worth mentioning of Latin or Greek." He had never been formally instructed in English: he had only the ordinary knowledge of arithmetic, and was altogether ignorant of English history and of biography. He knew, however, something of natural history, and had picked up the rudiments of physics, chemistry, and anatomy. Morally, he was extremely disobedient and contemptuous of authority; but naturally intelligent and of a kindly disposition.

At the age of thirteen Herbert was sent to

Hinton Charterhouse, near Bath, in order that his education might be carried on by his uncle, the Rev. Thomas Spencer, an advanced social reformer and temperance agitator. But he soon found the discipline more severe than he cared about, and ran away home to Derby again, walking forty-eight miles the first day, forty-seven the next, and twenty the third day, without sleep and with scarcely any food. He was, however, sent back to his uncle, with whom he subsequently got on satisfactorily. When he finally returned to Derby at the age of sixteen he had acquired a certain amount of mathematics, but was still very ignorant of languages and of history. He was, however, well set-up physically, and had undergone three years of a more rigorous discipline than that to which he was subjected in his father's house.

The following year, Spencer commenced his career as an assistant schoolmaster at Derby, but after three months' work with tolerable success a better opening presented itself. His uncle William obtained for him a post under Charles Fox, who was permanent resident engineer of one division of the London and Birmingham Railway, and forthwith he embraced the profession of a civil engineer. His salary was to begin at £80 a year ; but within a year his abilities had secured him a still better post as draughtsman on the Birmingham and Gloucester Railway at £120 a year, with headquarters at Worcester. His companions in his profession were not of a very elevating kind; but Spencer continued to be extremely steady, and his letters to his father at this period are mainly filled with various questions and suggestions on problems of mechanics. After a time he was further promoted to be engineering secretary to Captain Moorsom, who was engineer-in-chief of the line. He began to think of other things besides mathematics and engineering, and in April, 1840, wrote to his father : " I was thinking the other day that I should like to make public some of my ideas upon the state of the world and religion, together with a few remarks on education." For the time, however, his speculative tendencies were turned to invention. He devised a scale of equivalents, which was not published, and also a velocimeter for calculating velocities on railways, etc. More interesting was a meeting with a young lady of about his own age. For a few weeks they saw much of one another, and appear to have indulged in very mild flirtation. The association did not last long ; for the lady was engaged to someone else. The incident was of so light and transient a character that in no ordinary biography would it be worth mentioning. It is mentioned here only because this appears to have been the only occasion in Spencer's life when he ever experienced the attraction of the other sex.

The construction of the Birmingham and Gloucester Railway was finished in 1841, and the engineers employed upon it were discharged. The note in Spencer's diary " Got the sack—very glad " indicates his satisfaction on the recovery of his freedom. The hope of making something out of his inventions of various kinds led him to refuse a permanent appointment in the locomotive service, before even he had been informed what the duties were. He returned to his home at Derby with considerable savings, which he intended to devote to the prosecution of his inventions. Other interests of this period include natural history, the collection of fossils, modelling, and also phrenology.

The inventions, however, as usual came to nought ; and the year 1842 is interesting only on account of a series of letters written to an advanced dissenting organ called the *Nonconformist*. These letters, which bore the title " The Proper Sphere of Government," proposed to limit the functions of government entirely to the maintenance of justice. There was to be no provision for purposes of war, no restrictions on commerce, no poor laws, no national Church or national education, and no sanitary administration. The whole field of human activity was abandoned to private enterprise and voluntary co-operation. In the same year he embarked on active politics, and

became honorary secretary of the Derby branch
of the "Complete Suffrage Movement," which
was allied to the Chartist agitation.

These occupations, however, did not solve the
problem of earning a living, and in 1843 Spencer
decided to adopt a literary career and came up
to London to seek his fortune. He sent articles
to various reviews, but they were not accepted.
He spent over £10 in reprinting as a pamphlet
his articles on "The Proper Sphere of Government," but the proceeds of the first year's sales
amounted only to 14s. 3d. After three months
no literary engagement had turned up ; attempts
to find further employment at engineering were
equally fruitless, and at the end of 1843 Spencer
was obliged to return once more to Derby. After
several months of reading and writing, he was at
length offered the assistant editorship of a newspaper called the *Pilot*, which was about to be
established in Birmingham as an organ of the
Complete Suffrage Movement. The *Pilot* was
successfully launched after many difficulties, but
Spencer remained connected with it little more
than a month. An urgent invitation reached him
to assist in a survey of a proposed new branch
of the Birmingham and Gloucester Railway ; and
after some hesitation the proposal was accepted.
At this time Spencer was tolerably good-looking
in appearance, but brusque and self-assertive in

manner. His tendencies both in thought and politics were excessively radical; and apparently his advanced views about religion caused some lack of sympathy between him and his employer, Joseph Sturge, the editor of the *Pilot*. He was interested in philosophy, and even contemplated the founding of a paper to be called the *Philosopher;* but neither then nor afterwards did he ever undertake any serious course of reading on the subject. He tried to read Kant, but quickly threw him aside on the discovery that he disagreed with his first principles. As he often said in later life, idleness was a main characteristic of him, or, as would have stated the facts better, an ineptitude for discipline or for adhering to any course which failed to excite his interest.

The railway survey was succeeded by a visit to London, in order that the plans might be laid before the Committee on Standing Orders, with a view to passage through Parliament of a Bill authorising the construction of the new railway. The plans, however, were not accepted,—and with their rejection came a permanent end to Spencer's career as civil engineer. For two years he had no settled occupation, and spent nearly the whole of his time in devising various mechanical appliances; he gave some thought also to the plan of a new book in further development of the theories embodied in " The Proper Sphere of Government."

He had, however, no idea at this time of making authorship a profession.

Spencer's inventions were not more successful than inventions usually are. He spent some time in working out a machine for aerial locomotion ; but the difficulties were too great to be overcome. A " binding-pin," for fixing together the loose sheets of musical pieces or weekly periodicals, was attended with somewhat better success. It was placed upon the market, and the first sales gave ground for the belief that they would bring in a revenue of £70 a year. But when the novelty had worn off the sales soon came to an end. Spencer's prospects looked very gloomy, when towards the end of 1848 he was offered and accepted the appointment of sub-editor to the *Economist* at a salary of 100 guineas a year, with free bedroom and attendance at the offices of that newspaper, at 340, Strand. On the opposite side of the street was the publishing house of John Chapman with whom Spencer soon became acquainted. Chapman was in the habit of giving *soirées ;* and at these entertainments Spencer met many of those who in later life became his intimate friends. Among these was George Henry Lewes, with whom he carried on animated discussions about the then unfashionable " development hypothesis "—the theory that the organic world is a product of development, and not of creation.

Lewes introduced him to Carlyle; but their temperaments were too divergent to permit of friendship. At Chapman's *soirées*, also, Spencer made the acquaintance of Miss Mary Ann or Marian Evans, then chiefly known as the translatress of Strauss, and afterwards famous as George Eliot. Soon afterwards he met Huxley, who introduced him to Tyndall; and thus began two of the most intimate friendships of his life.

Spencer employed his spare time while at the *Economist* office in finishing his first book, which was published early in 1851 under the title of "Social Statics." Chapman was the publisher, but not unnaturally he declined to take any risks. Money was advanced for the purpose by one Woodfall, who printed it and who arranged to give Spencer two years' credit on the security of £80 which was still due to him, through the official liquidator, from one of the railway companies by which he had been employed. The book, which was dominated by the same idea as the articles on "The Proper Sphere of Government," was well received by the public; the theories which it contained were in harmony with the Radicalism of the time, and brought Spencer some reputation. Nevertheless his prospects remained very poor, and he seriously considered the question of emigration. With habitual method, he drew up a

list of the relative advantages of life in England
and in New Zealand ; each item being valued by
a number. England presented " greater domestic
comforts " valued at 10, " excitement in literature " valued at 20, " excitement in science "
at 6, and so on. On the other hand, New Zealand
offered the prospect of marriage, valued at 100.
In all, England summed up to 110 points, against
301 for New Zealand. No steps, however, were
taken to carry the idea into execution.

It is curious that at this time the idea of marriage should have occupied his mind. Spencer's
acquaintanceship with George Eliot had now
ripened into a close friendship. As sub-editor of
the *Economist* he received tickets giving free
admission for two persons to the theatres and
the Royal Italian Opera ; and during the early
months of 1852 he constantly took George Eliot
as his companion in these amusements, and
current gossip suggested that they were about to
be married. But this was not the case. Various
passages in Spencer's Autobiography convey the
notion that she was in love with him, but that he
was not in love with her. " There were reports
that I was in love with her, and that we were
about to be married. But neither of these reports
was true."[1] In a letter to a friend written at this
period he describes George Eliot as " the most

[1] Autobiography, i., 399.

admirable woman, mentally, I ever met "; and, as already mentioned, he then held marriage to be one of the most desirable consummations of life. The only clue to his attitude at this time is that furnished by a passage in the " Reflections " at the end of the Autobiography, where he says " Physical beauty is a *sine quâ non* with me ; as was once unhappily proved where the intellectual traits and the emotional traits were of the highest." [1]   I think there is no question whatever that the allusion here is to George Eliot ; and the conclusion to be drawn is that Spencer believed that George Eliot would have been willing to marry him.   But he himself had at this age, I do not doubt, lost any capacity he may have had for falling in love.

Spencer's book on " Social Statics " constituted an introduction to various reviews and periodicals. G. H. Lewes was then literary editor of a radical paper called the *Leader ;* and for this journal Spencer wrote a series of anonymous articles on a great variety of subjects under the title " The Haythorne Papers." The first was entitled " Use and Beauty "; the second dealt with " The Development Hypothesis "; others with Architectural Types, Gracefulness, etc.   The article on " The Development Hypothesis," is interesting on account of its advocacy of an evolution theory,

[1] Autobiography, ii., 445.

seven years before "The Origin of Species"
was published. The inheritance of acquired characters was named as the only and the adequate
cause of development; so that Spencer was at
this time more Lamarckian than Lamarck.
Most of these articles have been republished in
the Essays. In the same year, also, he wrote
an article for the *Westminster Review* on "A
Theory of Population," which was subsequently incorporated into "The Principles of
Biology."

In January, 1853, the Rev. Thomas Spencer
died, leaving over £500 to his nephew. With this
sum in hand, and with his new connections with
reviews, Spencer took the risk of resigning his
position on the *Economist*, hoping to earn a sufficient livelihood by writing miscellaneous articles.
He continued to write for the *Westminster Review*
and the *Leader;* and in 1854 wrote articles also
for the *North British Review*, the *British Quarterly
Review*, and the *Edinburgh Review*.

For five years Spencer had not been out of
London for more than four days at a time, with
the exception of one interval of ten days. He took
advantage of his new liberty, therefore, to make
a tour in Switzerland. Notwithstanding good
resolutions, he physically overtaxed himself walking and climbing; and on his return to London
signs of cardiac disturbance began, which never

afterwards left him, and which probably laid the foundation of his future ill-health.

In 1854 Spencer began to write his second book, " The Principles of Psychology." The reader of Spencer's life may not unnaturally inquire how it happened that from this time forward Spencer continued to write books on Philosophy, Biology, and Psychology, without having undergone any previous course of instruction in those subjects. It is indeed not easy to say how he acquired his information. As regards philosophy, he had read Lewes's " Biographical History of Philosophy "; and for the rest he appears to have glanced at a number of works on these subjects, picking up a little from each, but without any systematic course of study. His association with many who were destined to become famous in later years kept him constantly in an atmosphere of high intellectual character. But nearly all his books show, as might be expected, little connection with the lines of thought fashionable at the time. He came to each subject perfectly fresh, and thought out theories *de novo* for himself. " The Principles of Psychology," for example, dealt with the subject from an entirely new point of view. There can be no doubt that he lost much from ignorance of the work of his predecessors. There can be equally little doubt that he gained more by coming on the ground unbiassed and untrammelled by older

methods of looking at things. Most of the sciences
on which he wrote were in their infancy; and
it was possible at that time to write upon them
with very little previous knowledge. Moreover,
the commercial success which ultimately attended
his works is doubtless due in part to the fact that
he started from ground that was common to most
educated people, and could therefore be appreciated by the more intelligent of the general
public. Had his philosophy been based upon the
technical knowledge already known, it might
possibly have had a more enduring value, but
would certainly have had a less wide popular
appeal.

"The Principles of Psychology" was published
in 1855. No publisher would undertake any risks
in connection with it, and Spencer was obliged to
publish at his own expense. It met on the whole
with an antagonistic reception; and in particular
was made the subject of an article by R. H. Hutton
on "Modern Atheism" in the *National Review*,
a quarterly organ of the Unitarians. While it was
being written Spencer made various excu rsions—
one to Tréport, on the north coast of France,
another to Wales. It was during the latter excur-
sion that his health finally and permanently gave
way. The solitude entailed by hotel life led to
incessant thinking on the subject of his book,
until at length his nervous system broke down.

A peculiar sensation in the head seems to have been the only definite symptom ; but it involved an inability to sleep at night, which was never afterwards cured, and was probably the ultimate cause of his breakdown. For eighteen months he travelled from one country place to another in search of health, and in enforced idleness. As illustrating his nervous instability, he curiously mentions an occasion when his fishing-line got into a tangle, and induced him to give vent to an oath, which up to his present age of thirty-six he had never previously done. His wanderings at this time took him on one occasion to Paris, where he met the philosopher Comte, who did not greatly impress him.

At the end of 1856 Spencer returned to London. He had been advised by his doctor never again to live alone, and accordingly took up his residence as paying guest in a family at St. John's Wood. He recommenced work, though very slowly and laboriously, by an article for the *Westminster Review* on " Progress : Its Law and Cause," which embodied one of the leading ideas of " First Principles." In 1857 he collected a number of his essays together and republished them in a separate volume. It was apparently while preparing them for press that he was first taken by the idea of writing a System of Philosophy, which should gather together and co-ordinate the various heterogeneous

theories scattered throughout the " Essays " ; for
all of these were based upon a naturalistic interpretation of phenomena, and many of them had
reference to evolution. The scheme of the proposed
system was drawn up in the first week of 1858.
It was based upon the law of evolution, or, as he
then called it, the law of progress ; and was to
apply that law in the various departments of
science and philosophy ; in astronomy, geology,
biology, psychology, sociology, and ethics, or
rectitude, as he called it. Just six months after
the projection of this scheme Darwin and Wallace
read before the Linnæan Society their papers
announcing for the first time the doctrine of
Natural Selection.

The important question now at issue was how
Spencer should execute his project for a System
of Philosophy and at the same time earn a sufficient livelihood. He proposed to Chapman, in
whose hands the *Westminster Review* then was,
to publish the work in that periodical by quarterly
instalments, payment being made at the rate then
usual of ten guineas a sheet. But Chapman saw
no prospect of any profit to the *Westminster* from
such a course, and he declined. Writing to John
Stuart Mill about this proposal, he referred to
Spencer as being all brain and having " no heart."
Spencer then endeavoured to obtain the post of
stamp-distributor at Derby, which he thought

would leave him sufficient leisure for carrying out his purpose. With this object in view, he secured testimonials from Mill, Huxley, Tyndall, Grote, Hooker, Fraser, Sir Henry Holland, and Sir G. C. Lewis; but a Conservative Government was in power, and the office passed to one of the party adherents. At length it was decided to issue the work by quarterly instalments to subscribers, at the rate of 2s. 6d. for each instalment of 80—96 pages. Sixty-two subscribers, mostly of considerable distinction, were collected, and a circular was drawn up, containing this list of names and the programme of the proposed work, with an invitation to the public to subscribe. The circular was dated March 27, 1860; and in the course of the spring a total of between 300 and 400 subscribers was obtained, offering the promise of an income of £120 or £130 a year. Professor Edward L. Youmans, who afterwards projected the International Scientific Series, worked up the scheme in America, and succeeded in obtaining another 200 subscribers, so that the total at last reached 600. With this arrangement Spencer at the age of forty began to write the " Synthetic Philosophy."

The contract was kept neither by Spencer nor by his subscribers. It was not kept by Spencer, for a nervous relapse entailed a delay of three months in the issue of the first number; nor was it kept by the subscribers, whose subscriptions were often difficult to collect. The work was begun in a boarding-house in Bloomsbury, and carried on during frequent excursions to various parts of the country. Parts ii. and iii. were issued at the proper intervals, and then the smash of his printers involved him in an unexpected loss of £40 or £50. In the autumn of 1860, however, another uncle (William Spencer) died, and left him a legacy which enabled him for a time to continue his work. His health still remained exceedingly unsatisfactory, and he resorted to all sorts of methods to stave off cerebral congestion. He found great relief in dictating all his work to an amanuensis. Part of " First Principles " was written in a boat on the water in Regent's Park. Spencer would row for five minutes and then dictate for a quarter of an hour and so on. He also took his amanuensis to an open racquet court at Pentonville : he dictated the philosophy in a room near by, repairing to the racquet-court at frequent intervals to play a game or two and relieve the congestion of blood in the brain. The difficulties of making progress at length became so great that Spencer was ultimately obliged to issue a notice to the subscribers to the effect that each instalment would be issued when completed, without reference to regular dates. The book was at last finished in 1862 ; it attracted little attention. Such comments as were published by the newspapers were mainly devoted to criticism of the agnostic attitude of the metaphysical portion. The book was published on commission by Messrs. Williams and Norgate in England, and on a royalty of 15 per cent. by Messrs. Appleton in New York. This arrangement was adhered to in the case of all Spencer's subsequent writings.

Before "First Principles" was finished Spencer collected four essays, previously published in reviews, and re-issued them as a book entitled "Education." This work has had an enormous success, and is now translated into all the chief languages of the world, as well as into several of the minor languages.

Upon the conclusion of "First Principles" Spencer immediately proceeded to work on the next volume of the System of Philosophy, viz., vol. i. of "The Principles of Biology." It was written in many different places—in the Highlands of Scotland, in London boarding-houses, etc., and was finally published in 1864, but, like its predecessor, attracted little public attention. While engaged upon it he collected and republished a second series of his "Essays," but this also received scant notice in the Press. Shortly before the publication of vol. i. of "The Principles of Biology" Spencer took up his residence at a boarding-house at 88, Kensington Gardens Square.

In the same year, 1864, he published his essay on
the "Classification of the Sciences" as a *brochure*
with a postscript entitled "Reasons for Dissenting
from the Philosophy of M. Comte," both now
republished in vol. ii. of the "Essays." The
postscript was prompted by a suggestion in the
Revue des Deux Mondes that Spencer adhered to
the Positive Philosophy; he was always extremely
sensitive to any suggestion of indebtedness, either
to the views of Comte or anyone else. This sensitiveness is shown again by his repudiation of the
idea that Huxley and Hooker had supplied him
with his facts for "The Principles of Biology."
They did in fact read the proofs of that work and
make suggestions, for which acknowledgment is
made in the preface.

At the end of 1864 was founded the famous
x club, consisting of Spencer, Huxley, Tyndall,
Hooker, Lubbock (Lord Avebury), Frankland,
Busk, Hirst, and soon after, W. Spottiswoode.
It was a dining-club which met on the first Thurs-
day of every month, and exercised considerable
scientific influence, including, as it did, among its
members three who became President of the Royal
Society, five who became President of the British
Association, as well as a President of the College
of Surgeons and a President of the Chemical
Society.

The second volume of "The Principles of

Biology " was published in 1866. Spencer discovered that Alexander Bain had been deterred
from reading his previous works by deceptive
notices in the Press. He therefore decided not to
risk any further misrepresentation of the kind,
and the new volume was not sent out for review
at all. While engaged in its composition, he
carried out the only piece of practical research
work which he ever undertook. The subject of
it was the circulation of sap in plants ; the main
object was to show that the sap flowed through
the channels in the wood, and to offer suggestions
as to the mechanics of the process.

At the time when " The Principles of Biology "
was completed Spencer calculated that he had
sunk altogether nearly £1,100 in writing and
publishing books. He was obliged every year to
dip into the capital which he had acquired from
his two uncles : at length he was approaching an
end of his resources, and at the end of 1865 issued
to subscribers a notice of cessation. Many offers
of assistance were at once received. John Stuart
Mill wrote offering to guarantee the publishers
against any loss that might be incurred by a continuance of the work, etc. ; but Spencer remained
obdurate. A circular was then drawn up, without
Spencer's knowledge, and signed by Mill, Huxley,
Tyndall, Busk, and Lubbock (afterwards Lord
Avebury), inviting a wider public to subscribe to

the philosophic serial. Spencer assented very reluctantly to the issue of the circular ; but just at this moment the death of his father brought him once again a legacy, which relieved his situation, and he at once wrote to ask that the arrangements for its issue might be cancelled. Nevertheless the announcement of cessation of the serial had produced its effect. Professor Youmans in six months collected a considerable sum in America from Spencer's admirers. Aware that any direct presentation would certainly be declined, they invested 7,000 dollars in Spencer's name in public securities, so that he had no option of refusal ; at the same time they presented him with a handsome gold watch. Henceforward Spencer's circumstances became comparatively easy ; for his books soon after began to pay, and as they were all published on commission, the profits accrued directly to him. The death of his mother left him free from any embarrassments. During her illness he invented a new kind of invalid bed, which, however, never had any public popularity. He now settled himself to work steadily onwards with his philosophy. Refusing an invitation to stand for the Professorship of Mental Philosophy and Logic at University College, he went to live at a boarding-house at 37, Queen's Gardens, Lancaster Gate, taking also a room close by at 2, Leinster Place to serve as a study. Here he continued to live for nearly a quarter of a century. Henceforward there are few events in Spencer's life worth relating. In the critical year 1866 he had been an active member of the so-called Jamaica Committee for the prosecution of Governor Eyre—a Committee which included also the names of John Mill, Darwin, Huxley, and Wallace. But the consequent excitement had bad nervous effects, and he never again joined in any active public movement.

Spencer's first concern after the conclusion of " The Principles of Biology " was to prepare a second edition of " First Principles," incorporating some new ideas which had come to him while writing the essay on the Classification of the Sciences. The next business was to proceed with " The Principles of Psychology," based upon his earlier work, which was to form the next division of the System of Philosophy. But before embarking upon this work, Spencer had to make arrangements for acquiring a collection of facts on which to base the inductions of the later volumes on Sociology. The preparation for this work involved the perusal of immense numbers of books, describing the customs and organisation of primitive as well as civilised peoples ; and in 1867 Spencer engaged Dr. David Duncan (afterwards his biographer) to read books of travel and to select from them all statements that had any sociological interest, and to arrange them in accordance with a classification which Spencer had drawn up. In 1868 he was elected a member of the Athenæum Club under Rule 2, which empowers the committee to select from among the candidates nine each year who have attained to special eminence in science, literature, art, or public services. He was much gratified by his election, and thereafter became a very well-known member of the club, spending several hours there each day, and especially frequenting the billiard-room. The same year he made a tour in Italy, and while at Naples a pickpocket snatched his opera-glasses from his pocket. Spencer immediately started off in pursuit, and finally caught the thief and delivered him over to the police. In Rome he found plenty of scope for his independence of judgment and defiance of authority in criticising the works of the old masters, mainly on account of the technical and scientific errors in their productions.

" The Principles of Psychology " was based upon Spencer's earlier publication, with the addition of several new parts. Portions of this work were dictated in the intervals of rowing on the Serpentine, the boat being moored under the bushes when composition began. But Spencer still made frequent excursions to the country, and especially to Scotland, where he was fond of fishing. Incidentally he invented and published in the *Field* a description of a new form of joint for fishing-rods. The first volume of " The Principles of Psychology " was published in 1870 and the second in 1872. In that year his portrait was painted by J. B. Burgess, on behalf of Appleton, his American publisher, who wished to present it to some institution in New York.

In 1872–3 there occurred a temporary interruption in Spencer's philosophical work. His friend Professor Youmans, who had founded the International Scientific Series, pressed Spencer to write a volume for it, and he at length agreed to write on " The Study of Sociology." The chapters were published serially in the *Contemporary Review*, and Youmans endeavoured to arrange for simultaneous publication in some American review. His efforts were without success ; but, being a man of energy and determination, he promptly started a review of his own, in which Spencer's articles might be published. In this way was born the *Popular Science Monthly*, which has had a long and successful career. The book itself was issued at the end of 1873 and turned out to be remarkably popular. It was sold for 5*s*., and altogether Spencer made a net profit of more than £1,500 from the articles and book together. The articles, moreover, stimulated the sale of all his other works.

Dr. Duncan had now so far advanced with his work of compilation of sociological facts that the

first volume of "The Descriptive Sociology"
was published in 1873, and the next year it
was followed by the second volume. In 1870 Dr.
Duncan had been appointed Professor of Logic at
Madras, and his work was taken over by Mr. James
Collier. In the following year Youmans pressed
Spencer to accelerate the work by appointing an
additional compiler, undertaking that the ex-
penses should be defrayed by American admirers.
Accordingly an advertisement in the German
Press brought an answer from Dr. Richard
Scheppig, who thereafter continued the work in
addition to Mr. Collier. The financial arrangement
with Youmans, however, was not carried out.
Spencer's meticulous pride and fear of misrepresentation led him to reject the proposal for reim-
bursement by the Americans, notwithstanding that
the issue of the first number cost him nearly
£700, and the proceeds of the sale were very small.
A second and independent offer of £500 from an
actuary of St. Louis to enable the work to be
continued was similarly declined. In all, eight
folio volumes of "The Descriptive Sociology"
were published before the heavy losses involved
compelled a cessation of publication in 1881. The
work consists of series of large tables of classification of sociological facts, succeeded by a great
number of extracts from books of travel, on which
the tables are based. They are therefore quite

unsuitable for general reading. At the time of cessation the total loss on the undertaking, without reckoning the loss of interest on money sunk, was about £3,250.

The tabulation of facts had proceeded far enough by 1874 to enable Spencer to begin his " Principles of Sociology " when he had finished with " The Study of Sociology." It was issued to the subscribers in the ordinary way during the following three years, and vol. i. was ultimately published as a volume in 1877. By this time the philosophic serial had run to forty-four numbers ; and as there no longer appeared any reason to continue the serial form of publication a notice was sent out to the effect that thenceforward the volumes would only be published when completed. With vol. i. of " The Principles of Sociology " Spencer resumed the habit of sending out copies of his works for review.

His next task was to proceed with vol. ii. opening with an account of " Ceremonial Institutions." An arrangement was made with Mr. John Morley to publish the successive chapters as articles in the *Fortnightly Review;* but so little public interest was excited in them that the arrangement was soon brought to an end. " Ceremonial Institutions " was published as a separate volume in 1879. At this time Spencer's health was so greatly reduced that he had reason to fear he would never be able to reach the end of his under-

taking. He therefore decided to drop the remainder
of " The Principles of Sociology " for the present
and to start upon the final work, " The Principles
of Morality," " since the whole system was at the
outset, and has ever continued to be, a basis for
a right rule of life, individual and social." The
name *Ethics* was substituted for that of *Morality*,
and the first portion of " The Principles of Ethics "
was published under the title of " The Data of
Ethics " in 1879. So anxious was Spencer to
make progress with this part of the work that he
postponed the publication of " Ceremonial Institutions " until " The Data of Ethics " was already
out.

During the latter half of Spencer's life his hours
of work were limited to three or four a day. After
1 or 2 o'clock he was unable to sit down to any
work requiring attention, under the penalty of
having an altogether sleepless night. Even novel-
reading, of which he was very fond, was too
stimulating for him, and he resorted to all kinds of
methods for killing time during the greater part of
the day. One expedient adopted for this purpose
was the preparation and dictation of his Autobiography, begun in 1875. If, therefore, we are
inclined to criticise that work on account of its
unwieldy size and somewhat tedious self-analysis
and relation of trifles, we should remember that it
represents the desperate efforts of a confirmed

invalid to find occupation during long hours of weariness.

On the publication of " Ceremonial Institutions " Spencer joined some friends on a tour to Egypt and up the Nile. His ill-health, however, prevented the enjoyment of the trip ; dyspepsia gave rise to a mild form of delusions, which caused him to hasten back to Cairo before reaching the end of his voyage on the Nile. He returned home by Venice, remarking of St. Mark's that it was " a fine sample of barbaric architecture." He was greatly pleased on arriving once more in England and being able to continue his former work.

With the completion of " The Data of Ethics " he returned to the next division of " The Principles of Sociology." This division was issued, like the previous one, in a series of articles for the *Fortnightly Review*, simultaneously published in the *Popular Science Monthly*, and in various foreign European reviews. The volume was issued in 1882 ; and at the same time it was bound up with the previous work on " Ceremonial Institutions," and the two together were re-issued as vol. ii. of " The Principles of Sociology " and vol. vii. of " The Synthetic Philosophy." About this time Spencer was active in assisting in the foundation of a new society called the Anti-Aggression League, in which he was associated with Mr. Frederic Harrison, Mr. John Morley, and others. The

object of the League was to try and prevent
aggressive wars on primitive peoples; for he
regarded most of our colonial wars in this light.
Nothing came of the movement, however; and
the excitement had so bad an effect on Spencer's
health that he never permanently recovered from
it.

In the autumn of 1882 he paid a visit to America.
Numerous attempts were made to *fête* him, but
he exercised the greatest care to preserve his
incognito; and once only in New York was he
entertained at a banquet. He prepared himself for
the ordeal with the utmost care; waited in an
ante-room near by until the last moment before
dinner when it was necessary for him to appear;
and during dinner requested his neighbour to talk
to him as little as possible. His carefully-prepared
speech was delivered without much effect or
oratorical power : the burden of it was that life
was not for work or for money-making, but that
work and money-making were the means, easily
overdone, of leading a fuller and happier life. He
declined as much as £300 for a lecture, saying that
he was wholly unaccustomed to lecturing, and that
to do so " would be nothing more than making
myself a show; and I absolutely decline to make
myself a show."

Soon after his return to England Spencer
started upon a crusade against the political move-

ment which was then beginning towards an increase in the functions and activities of the State as opposed to the individual. In 1884, four trenchant articles on this subject appeared in the *Contemporary Review*, which were afterwards bound together and issued under the title of "The Man *versus* the State." The next occupation was to proceed with the third volume of "The Principles of Sociology," and in 1885 the first part of this was published separately under the title "Ecclesiastical Institutions." The final chapter of this work, entitled "Religious Retrospect and Prospect," was published independently in the *Nineteenth Century*, and immediately gave rise to a vigorous controversy with Mr. Frederic Harrison. Spencer had contended that the religion of the future would take the form of a contemplation of the mysteries of the Unknowable ; Mr. Harrison, on the other hand, urged the religion of humanity. Youmans wrote to Spencer from America, emphasising the need for republishing the succession of articles in book form in that country. This accordingly was done, under the editorship of Professor Youmans, and including also a general review of the controversy by the Count Goblet d'Alviella. "The Nature and Reality of Religion," as the volume was called, was published by Messrs. Appleton in the spring of 1885 ; and a copy was sent to Mr. Harrison, who immediately wrote to

Spencer to ask why his permission had not been
sought before the re-publication of his share of the
controversy. This letter was followed two days
later by a letter of protest to *The Times*, under
the title of " A New Form of Literary Piracy."
Although the American copyright law furnished
no protection whatever to authors who published
in England, yet a moral claim was always recognised by the leading American publishers, including, of course, Messrs. Appleton. Moreover, seeing
that Youmans had written for the book a strongly
Spencerian introduction and had appended hostile
notes to the articles of Mr. Harrison, it was perfectly clear that Mr. Harrison had an eminently
legitimate grievance. After some days Spencer
recognised the unfortunate error that had been
made, and cabled to New York to have the book
suppressed—which was immediately done. Mr.
Harrison behaved to Spencer throughout with
the greatest courtesy and consideration ; and
there seems no reason why Spencer should have
felt any animosity for a mistake which was entirely
due to himself and his friends. An unauthorised
and piratical edition was afterwards brought out
in Boston. An account of the book is included
in Chap. VIII.

In 1886 Spencer published in the *Nineteenth
Century* his articles on " The Factors of Organic
Evolution," affirming the inheritance of acquired

characters, and the inadequacy of natural selection to account for all the phenomena of evolution. Up to this date he had continued to live in the same boarding-house near Lancaster Gate ; but he was beginning to feel the necessity of a more commodious residence, and in 1889 he took a house at 64, Avenue Road, St. John's Wood, with three maiden ladies. Meanwhile he continued to work at the System of Philosophy. On the completion of " Ecclesiastical Institutions " he decided once again to abandon " The Principles of Sociology," until he should have finished his last and more important work on Ethics. On turning to this task, he began with the most important division on " Justice," which was published in 1891. In 1892 the first volume of " The Principles of Ethics " was completed, and the year following the second volume including " Justice " appeared.

In 1889 there occurred an unfortunate incident which temporarily broke Spencer's long friendship with Huxley. A correspondence in *The Times* on Land Nationalisation turned in part upon Spencer's views on that subject. As a young man he had been warmly in favour of that policy, which, indeed, he had advocated in the original edition of " Social Statics." But later on he had come to the conclusion that, although nationalisation of the land was equitable from the point

of view of Absolute Ethics, yet the economic
difficulties were so great that in the view of
Relative Ethics such a change was in practice
undesirable.   Huxley intervened in the controversy, scoffing at the conception of any Absolute
Ethics; and the result of the controversy was an
estrangement, which was exacerbated the following year by another controversy in the *Daily
Telegraph* of the same character. The difference
was not made up till 1893. In that year and
the following year Spencer was busy with his
controversy with Weismann on the inheritance of
acquired characters; and then he turned his
attention to the conclusion of the Synthetic
Philosophy.   There remained only the third
volume of " The Principles of Sociology " to be
completed, and this was published in 1896. A
chorus of public congratulation followed.   Sir
Joseph Hooker addressed to him a letter signed by
eighty-two of the most distinguished representatives of science and literature, requesting him
to sit for his portrait with a view to its presentation to one of the national collections. He had
already once declined to sit for a portrait by
Millais ; but the present invitation was too strong
to be resisted, and it was arranged that the portrait
should be painted by Mr. (afterwards Sir) Hubert
von Herkomer.   But Spencer was too impatient,
and his health was too bad, to allow of satis-

factory sittings, and the portrait was only a moderate success.

From this time forwards Spencer's life must have been singularly unhappy. His health went from bad to worse, and the valetudinarianism into which he was forced led to a heightened egoism, in which his thoughts were turned permanently and almost without relief upon himself. He became exceedingly irritable and sensitive, and was largely preoccupied with rebutting charges of indebtedness for his ideas to previous authors. A man whose emotional tendencies had been drained off into philosophical studies, he seemed largely to have lost the capacity for personal affection; he was ready to quarrel with almost any friend; his life was bound up in the advocacy of his philosophical opinions. And unfortunately the current of opinion was running every year more strongly against his views. In Biology he witnessed the gradual decline in favour of his favourite theory of the Inheritance of Acquired Characters. More trying still was the rapid advance in England towards Militarism and towards Socialism, against which the main doctrines of his Social Philosophy were exclusively directed. Moreover, it is impossible to study his works closely without perceiving a marked deterioration both in his powers of thought and in his literary style. As regards the former, he did little more

than follow up mechanically the conceptions
which he had entertained in youth. As regards the
latter, he became pompous, and, if he had been a
lesser man, it might even have been added prig-
gish. A clue to the deterioration may perhaps be
found in a sentence in his preface to the Autobiography : " in the genesis of a system of thought
the emotional nature is a large factor." But
Spencer became emotionally barren ; the Synthetic Philosophy alone was too abstract and
unsubstantial to provide adequate outlet for the
deep feelings of a vigorous constitution. His
emotions withered from lack of sustenance ; and
his powerful mind became concentrated on the
minute trivialities of a common-place life. So
deeply did these trivialities obsess him that at
the end of his life he even condescended to write
for the information of posterity a detailed account
of the state of his teeth, the age at which they
had begun to decay, etc.

The French have a saying that " La Vanité est
l'ennemi du bonheur." Vanity is but one of the
manifestations of egoism ; and egoism is the fate
of those who have lost the capacity for the more
massive emotions. When the mind is by nature
powerful, the degradation is the more overwhelming and complete. *Corruptio optimi pessima.*
Spencer can never have been a truly happy man.
Even in the thirties he had reached the conclusion

that, notwithstanding all his personal advantages, life was scarcely worth living; and it is curious to note the immediate and energetic repudiation of this utterance by Lewes and George Eliot, in whose presence it was made. What was then a mere absence of happiness became later a complete domination of wretchedness. It may perhaps be said that the deepest distinction between youth and age is that the former is devoted to the pursuit of pleasure, the latter to the avoidance of pain. If Spencer never achieved the former, he still more completely failed in meeting the latter condition. Yet the true philosopher will not regard him with blame. The physiological tax entailed by the origination of a great system of thought may well account for weakness elsewhere.

Spencer had now lived for some years at 64, Avenue Road, but on April 1, 1897, he decided to terminate the agreement with the three ladies who lived there with him. "All things considered," he wrote to them, "I do not desire any longer to maintain our relations. . . . On estimating the advantages I derive from the presence of yourself and your sisters in the house, I find them but small—not by any means great enough to counterbalance the disadvantages." And so he gave them three months' notice to leave. After a short stay in the country he took chambers in London near the

Athenæum, but after three days he broke down and returned for another few months to the house in Avenue Road where he was now alone. Dislike of the solitude and monotony, however, caused him at the end of the year to change his abode altogether, and at the beginning of 1898 he took a house at 5, Percival Terrace, Brighton, where he hoped many of his friends from London would visit him, and where in any case the monotony would be relieved by more sunlight and the prospect of the sea. Here he engaged two ladies to complete his domestic circle—one to act as housekeeper and the other as pianist ; for music remained as almost the last pleasure of his life.

The remainder of Spencer's life was spent in dreary emptiness, preoccupied to a great extent with clearing up misrepresentations of his doctrines or ascriptions of his ideas to previous writers. But as he said himself, after fifty years of a literary life it was impossible altogether to give up the habit of writing books ; and on April 25, 1902, he published a volume of short essays under the title of " Facts and Comments." His ill-health prevented him from giving more than a few minutes' dictation every day to the writing of this book ; and, as it was definitely announced as his last, considerable public attention was attracted to it. At length he began to be overwhelmed by his infirmities, symptoms of aphasia presented themselves, and he died early in the morning of December 8, 1903. He was cremated at Golder's Green without any religious ceremony. By his own previous instructions no mourning was worn and a secular address was delivered by Mr. Leonard (now Lord) Courtney. The ashes were subsequently buried in Highgate Cemetery.

CHAPTER III

In his Autobiography Spencer has attempted to analyse his own mental characteristics; but it cannot be said that the attempt was altogether a success. For although that work certainly provides a valuable picture of the man, yet the value is not so much in the conscious analysis as in the unconscious style: the things which he thought worth while setting down and the way in which he said them. Spencer was too much addicted to self-analysis to describe himself in a way that would interest other people. He was too prone to set down what interested himself, and analysis by an outsider will bring out many points which he scarcely perceived himself. Let us follow his own plan and deal with his physical characteristics first.

He was 5 feet 10 inches in height; and though his constitution did not appear to be robust, yet he had none of the appearance of a confirmed invalid. He was particularly proud of his hands, and when he was seventy-eight had a plaster-cast taken of them, which is now in the public museum at Derby. They were of smaller size than usual;

and he was fond of using this fact in illustration of the theory of inheritance of acquired characters. His ancestors for some generations back had done no manual labour (a circumstance of which, I think, he was inclined to be vain); their hands, therefore, had not been largely developed, and he had been born with hands congenitally smaller than usual.

He was also somewhat vain of his teeth; and it is indeed remarkable that through all his long life he never had one taken out or stopped. So much we are informed in the official Life by Dr. Duncan; but Spencer himself has recorded that as he got older many of his teeth were badly decayed; and it would have been very much better for him if he had foregone his dental prejudices and had them properly attended to. In the light of recent theories it may even be surmised that the condition of Spencer's health was in great degree contributed to by the unhygienic state of his teeth.

The origin of his illness has been recorded by Spencer with minute detail in his Autobiography. It appears to have been an uncommon form of neurasthenia, of which the most conspicuous symptom was inability to sleep at night. He himself believed that the fundamental cause was congestion of the blood in the brain; and in documents hitherto unpublished he attributes his breakdown in great part to exercises which he took in violent breathing, in the hope that he might derive from it some benefit.

The result of this nervous condition was that he was never able to do any work or carry on exciting conversation after the middle of the day without paying the penalty of a sleepless night. Even novel-reading for more than a few minutes at a time was an excitement which he had to forego. It was in view of the necessity of avoiding any form of excitement that he carried with him a pair of ear-pads connected together by a spring passing round the back of his head. Sir Ray Lankester relates how, when he was quite a young man, Spencer asked him to call to see him at the Athenæum to give him some information about certain biological matters. On arriving, Spencer expounded to Sir Ray his own theories with regard to the matters in question. But as soon as Sir Ray began to point out one or two difficulties, Spencer hastily closed the conversation by fitting on his ear-pads, saying that his medical advisers would not allow him to enter into discussions.

This same neurasthenia likewise caused Spencer to develop a habit to which for some reason his biographers have paid very little attention, namely, that of the regular taking of opium. Soon after he was forty he took morphia at occasional intervals in order to restore the periodicity of sleep ;

and as an older man he contracted the habit of invariably taking one and a half grains of opium every night. He defends the practice on the ground that there is an unreasonable fear of this drug, which when not abused is of great value. But it seems a question whether taking it regularly even in small quantities does not constitute an abuse, and may not have been another contributory cause of his shattered nervous system. Of his physical characteristics it only remains to add that, apart from his peculiar complaint, he had a strong constitution, and, though somewhat lacking in muscular strength, was in his youth a good walker and runner.

Mentally, Spencer's most obvious characteristic was his extreme originality and dislike of authority or convention. He was by nature a rebel; in early manhood he was well described by one of his friends as " radical all over." But as he got older this trait lost its fluidity : on the one hand it hardened into dogma, while on the other hand he respected the conventions in reality far more than he would have cared to admit. In all those matters on which he rebelled during youth he adhered to his attitude and became, as it were, a heretic on principle. But in other matters to which he had given little attention in youth he was not inclined to become heretical in later years ; and his behaviour in society was much like that

of ordinary middle-class people. For it must be
noted that, in appearance and conversation, the
bourgeoisie was tolerably conspicuous. In those
spheres of conduct where his philosophic principles had nothing to say, he tended even to be
representative of the Bayswater boarding-houses,
where his inclination led him to spend so large
a portion of his life.

Yet Spencer was a man of immensely strong
individual personality. There can be little question
that this was the basis of his doctrine of social
freedom. He could not bear to have his liberty
of thought or action curtailed in any kind of way.
His personality was everywhere intruded, and
could suffer no limitations and live under no
compulsion. And this fact partly explains how
he—a singularly idle man—came to write so many
learned volumes. It was all part of his expanding
personality ; or, if we like to put it so, an immense
monument of egoism. And this same fact also
explains another striking characteristic of his
mind, the utter lack of receptivity. He was always
a very small reader ; he can scarcely ever have
sat down to learn something new, and the books
which he read were those which were agreeable
to him, either from intrinsic interest or on account
of their harmony with his own views. He often
boasted how he had never read more than a few
pages of Kant, and had thrown aside the works

of that philosopher as soon as he came upon a conclusion with which he disagreed. And he applied the same principle, or gave in to the same weakness, throughout.

His methods of work again illustrate an almost morbid exaggeration of personality. Men of science and philosophers commonly set before themselves some problem to be solved, and proceed to work up the facts all round it with the view of finding the solution. Spencer never did anything of the kind. His system of thought grew up organically inside him. His network of principles gradually enmeshed one after another of the common problems of the time; but until this expanding network reached them naturally he took no interest either in them or their solution: they were outside his sphere altogether. He could not read Kant from the same mental peculiarity that he could not have a tooth extracted: in both cases a subtraction from his own personality was involved. For the same organic reason he was a deadly opponent of militarism. How could such a man have supported the restrictions of a soldier's life? How could he have sunk himself to be a mere unit in a drilling regiment? As Renan said of himself, he would either have deserted or committed suicide. Let not our criticisms be too severe. If some persons cannot be forced into our mould, we must consider whether after all it is wise that there should only be one mould into which everyone must go.

From these mental features monoideism is another corollary. Spencer's mind was obsessed, as already explained, by a few general principles in accordance with which he conducted his entire life and fabricated his entire system of thought. In the subjects which fell within those principles he had extraordinary power and insight—truly wonderful gifts : in the subjects which fell without their scope he was just the ordinary man in the street, the suburban owner of a semi-detached villa. We have all heard at times of the astounding achievements of persons (sometimes of inferior intellect or even feeble-minded) whose minds are wholly limited to one idea. The achievements of Spencer are of that order—the supernatural acuity of vision endowed by the most overwhelming intellectual concentration.

Spencer was systematical and methodical in all walks of life. As a young man he took naturally to mechanics ; and his whole system of thought is based on a mechanistic or naturalistic way of looking at things. Mathematics naturally appealed to him ; for it proceeds by the deductive method from a few simple premises. And the branch of mathematics in which he took the greatest interest was geometry. We may suspect that he belonged to the psychological type or strong visualisers. His philosophy is in many respects Euclidean in form, and his scheme of phenomena is such as may be *seen* in imagination ; the world is laid out on the pattern of a geometrical diagram.

Emotionally Spencer was somewhat cold. Allusion has already been made to an unpublished letter from John Chapman, the publisher, to John Stuart Mill, written when Spencer was about forty, in which Chapman refers to Spencer as having " no heart," but as being totally consumed by his extraordinary intellect. It would, however, be incorrect to say that he did not feel deeply, for in fact he was exceedingly sensitive. In the preface to his Autobiography he observes " that in the genesis of a system of thought the emotional nature is a large factor : perhaps as large a factor as the intellectual nature." As already explained, his whole energy, emotional as well as intellectual, was absorbed in the *principles* around which he constituted his life and philosophy. He had not much feeling for persons, for the same reason that ascetics and martyrs have little feeling for persons. Thus we have the strange circumstance that he practically did not know what it meant to fall in love. Marriage appealed to him as an abstract proposition, but he never found any temptation to it in the concrete. In matters of sex he carried prudishness to an extreme degree. The principles of his social philosophy did not embrace any sexual problems ; they never occupied any perceptible share of his attention ; and being, as it were, outside his philosophy, his views on sex were just those of a middle-class dissenting minister in the most rigid period of Victorian banality. Although there was a deep strain of the puritan and ascetic in Spencer, yet he was exceedingly intolerant of minor discomforts. He appeared to be acutely sensitive, and in various ways laid himself out to procure enjoyments. There is no sort of asceticism in his philosophy : his ethics are professedly hedonistic ; and he often condemned both in writing and speaking those who took a severe view of the pursuit of happiness. But one thing seems certain : that if he aimed at happiness in theory he scarcely achieved it in practice. Even when young and prosperous, he doubted whether life was worth living ; when old and invalided, he found life a perpetual round of weariness and misery. Perhaps this peculiarity is best explained by his non-emotional type of character ; for happiness resides, not in sensation nor in intellect but in emotion : and no philosophical principles can induce emotion where there is naturally little.

If it has to be added that Spencer was both vain and egotistical, I am merely naming traits which go necessarily with those already mentioned. Yet both these flaws were in him entirely venial and free from the unpleasant social results commonly associated with them. This was in part due to the fact that his good opinion of himself was entirely justified by the very eminent qualities which he plainly possessed ; but still more to the fact that they were completely dissociated from any form or suggestion of affectation. Spencer was pre-eminently simple and unadorned in manner : his judgment of other people's characters was similarly guileless ; in this respect he scarcely rose above the capabilities of an average clergyman or schoolmaster. Probably of all human weaknesses affectation was that most foreign to his character. He was sincere to the last degree : the most absolute sincerity characterised not only his philosophic opinions, but his every action and utterance in the smallest detail of life and conversation. Shallow people are very apt to attribute all kinds of eccentricity or breaches of convention as springing from affectation : they do so because in their own cases their only temptation to heterodoxy is from affectation ; and nearly all men commit the error of judging others by themselves. But Spencer's mind was wholly different from the common run ; and those who will attempt to understand his motives by reference to their own would be well advised to relinquish the study of him without delay.

Spencer's sincerity was the occasion of some deficiency of social tact. The man who in any society will invariably say precisely what he thinks is something of an *enfant terrible*, and apt to be occasionally misunderstood. This result is still more emphatic when what he thinks happened so often to be entirely opposed to what anybody else thought. But there was not a spark of self-suppression in Spencer's constitution. To tell a lie, or even to appear by his silence to acquiesce in statements with which he really disagreed, were contrary to the deepest instincts of his nature. And all this, be it observed, is bound up with his fundamental love of freedom. When society is free and tolerant, the average truthfulness is high. It is a well-known principle of education that the least truthful children are those who have been subjected to the most coercive methods. Men are born unlike ; and they always remain unlike, at least in the minor affairs of belief and conduct. No coercion can reduce them to real similarity, though it can and does easily reduce them to the outward appearance of similarity. In proportion as society is tolerant of divergences from the normal, there remains small occasion to conceal such divergences. But in proportion as society insists upon a rigid conformity, the innate differences will be, not abolished, but concealed, and the general state of truthfulness will suffer.

Spencer was somewhat cold or " stand-offish " among strangers—a feature which arose partly from shyness and partly from a natural dignity. Although little accustomed to restrain expressions of opinion or feeling, he never appeared excited, and was rarely betrayed into unparliamentary or rather unphilosophic language. In the Autobiography he relates indeed one occasion when he was betrayed into " venting an oath." The cause of his irritation, as already related, was when his fishing-line had got into a tangle—a time when swearing is surely venial if not actually desirable. Tyndall once said of him what a much better fellow he would be if he had a good swear now and again. But Spencer's feelings were rarely of the kind that may be relieved by swearing.

It remains to be added that Spencer was by nature an exceedingly idle man. His education had been singularly free from coercion and lacking in the customary discipline of authority. He had all his life been free; and after he grew up he never attempted to discipline himself. His knowledge arose, not from set studies, but from the possession of wide general principles which drew in cognate facts like magnets acting on iron filings. And perhaps one of the most singular peculiarities

of his mind was its extraordinary power to see the
essential elements in any heterogeneous mixture
of events.   He carved out a principle, which
immediately introduced order and method, where
previously there had been nothing but a hopeless
jumble.   Galton describes Spencer's mental workings in a vivid manner [1] :—

"The power of Spencer's mind that I most admired,
was that of widely-founded generalisations.   Whenever
doubt was hinted as to the sufficiency of his grounds for
making them, he was always ready to pour out a string
of examples that seemed to have been, if not in his
theatre of consciousness when he spoke, at all events in
an ante-chamber of it, whence they could be summoned
at will."

This is another form in which his passion for
principles appeared.   Psychologically it was based
on a power to detect fundamental resemblances—
or "association by similarity."   A medley of
facts would thus be quickly classified and hung up
on horizontal poles, as it were, as the principles
evolved out of them.   To this single capacity are
traceable all his powers of analysis, synthesis,
generalisation, etc.

His methods of thinking and writing were
wholly conformable with his character.   He no
more thought of sitting down to think than he
thought of sitting down to read.   In the course of
promiscuous idling he would come across some

[1] Duncan, p. 502.

significant fact or idea. which **very** likely he would temporarily forget. But later on it would be liable to turn up in his mind again, well on the way to being a full-fledged principle. And once the principle got rooted, relevant facts would come flying in from all quarters, until on all that subject quite a considerable amount of knowledge had been more or less unintent onally accumulated. These processes apparently occurred with special strength while taking walks : on these occasions he **was often** absent-minded and noticed little of what **was** going on about him. He had of course immense natural concentration, but it was never brought **on** by an effort of will.

His method of writing was of the same kind. The written matter flowed naturally from him, without conscious effort, and it was very little revised after being written. Unlike John Stuart Mill, who wrote out his Logic many times before he was satisfied with it, Spencer never re-wrote : his first copy was what went to the printers, though he made a number of minor alterations in the proofs. All this came partly from natural idleness, and partly from the fact that his mental concentration, being involuntary, could scarcely be brought a second time over precisely the same subject. The great majority of his works were dictated : this he found a great relief ; the dissi-pation of muscular effort in writing was saved for the unconscious mental effort. He could take up this dictation at almost any moment—in the intervals of rowing on the Serpentine, or of playing games of racquets with his amanuensis.

His style, as may be supposed, is singularly easy and fluent. In his earlier essays it was also vigorous and redeemed by flashes of humour. But later on it became less fluid : it hardened into an almost deadly monotony, and an outward symbol of the wooden dogmatism into which he gradually sank. But it always remained exceedingly lucid. As William James truly remarked of his mind, it had not the lights and shades of an ordinary style, it was a remorseless glare throughout. The oratorical passages which occur from time to time are often powerful, and arose from profound conviction and intense feeling of the truth of what he wrote. For the settled calmness of Spencer's mind was susceptible of occasional elevation. Even *his* self-confidence had its moments of maximum intensity.

It is well known that Spencer throughout his life refused all honours offered him, whether by universities, Governments, or scientific bodies. This was due in large part to pique ; for honours only came to him comparatively late in life. As he had no sort of official position, nor even a university degree, his success in the world naturally came later than is usual in the case of those

who start their careers under the ægis of universities and along the regular paths. A remarkable
personality backed by immense natural powers
will tell in the end; but public recognition is
necessarily slower than with those who are brought
by their positions before the public eye. After
he had written his " Principles of Psychology "
he no doubt thought that he had a strong claim
to be elected a fellow of the Royal Society. But
that honour was not offered him till much later in
life, at a time when all his contemporaries had
become senior fellows; and he would have been
ranked with men a generation younger, and far
less distinguished, than himself. He was not
offered it, in fact, until his reputation was securely
established beyond dispute; and he felt that if
they declined to help him when he most needed
it there was no reason why he should acquiesce in
their authority when he could no longer derive
any advantage from it. Just as in the sphere of
action a rolling-stone usually comes to no good,
but on rare occasions becomes more famous than
any of the official hierarchy, so in the sphere of
thought a free-lance is usually worthless, but *may*
ultimately attain a distinction unknown to his
official contemporaries. In both cases the pre-
sumption is so much against the individualist that
recognition is usually long delayed. The departure
from the normal is usually a departure for the

bad. Not in one case out of a thousand is it really an improvement; but then it is apt to be an improvement of revolutionary importance— such as was certainly the case with Spencer. Spencer, having begun by refusing honours, could not well change his attitude when they began to be crowded quickly on him. He no doubt felt flattered at the thought that his success had been achieved solely by personal merit; and there is an undoubted distinction in surpassing the reputation of nearly all his contemporaries without any sort of handle to his name, such as they possessed in abundance.

Moreover, Spencer was by nature a republican and averse to all forms of social distinction. He would at any period of life have refused honours offered by the Government, on the ground that it was no part of the functions of government to award praise or blame to citizens; and in fact that they were not fit judges, at all events in the realm of philosophy. It is true that as he grew older he abandoned republican views, at least as regards society in its present condition. He expressed the opinion that it was no more right to deprive the people of their king than it was right to deprive a child of its doll. But his independent spirit could not enter easily into the social hierarchy; nor could he ever have suffered the thought that, by acceptance of a title, he acquiesced in a

position of inferiority to those who had higher
titles. The sentiment was far commoner then
than it is now ; but we cannot deny to it a genuine
dignity, and in any case it is a sentiment that is
not likely to be harboured by little men.

Spencer was more than once invited to stand
for Parliament ; but his opinions were much too
individual and much too uncompromising to
admit of his accepting such invitations. Socially
he had a great attraction towards club life, which
was eminently suited to his disposition. To those
whose minds naturally rebel against formalities
and restrictions clubs offer an ideal social resort.
There are no ties as to hours or appointments :
it is possible to go in at any time as inclination
prompts ; to read, write, or talk at will ; to make
friendships with many people, and to keep them
up by constant intercourse without pre-arrange-
ment ; to leave at any moment, and to speak more
freely than in society outside. There are no restrictions as to dress, and no conventions beyond
those which are essential in all social life. Clubs, in
fact, offer the freest possible form of society, and
as such strongly commended themselves to Spencer.
He belonged both to the Athenæum and the Savile.
Of the former he was for many years a most regular
habitué ; and his service on the committee was the
only approximation to administrative duties that
he was ever really interested in. His election to

the Savile did not take place till he was older:
he joined it partly, perhaps wholly, because he
could play billiards there on Sunday, which was
and is still interdicted by the ecclesiastical prejudices of the Athenæum. Although the Savile
society was in many ways more amusing and not
less distinguished than that of the Athenæum, he
never went there sufficiently to get in touch with it.
The members were younger, and far less reverent:
and they were certainly less imbued with the Victorian spirit, of which he was perhaps the most
typical representative.

Billiards was his favourite recreation in his
clubs. He attained a passable proficiency, and
has defended the pastime on philosophic grounds
from the frowns of Victorian puritanism. But he
did not care for cards, and was a bad whist-player.
Again on philosophic grounds he objected to
gambling; and when he played cards he would
always pay his losses but decline to receive his
winnings. It is worth while pointing out that
Spencer's argument against gambling is founded
on a logical fallacy which has occasionally been
repeated in text-books of logic. Supposing (as
in the case of Mr. Micawber) that a man has an
income of twenty pounds a year. Then if by
gambling he takes the risk of gaining or losing one
pound, he must (argued Spencer) on the whole be
a sufferer. For as a man's income increases each

additional pound is of less value to him than the last. The twenty-first pound in a man's income is of less value to him than the twentieth pound. The privation involved by reducing an income from twenty pounds to nineteen pounds is greater than the advantage accruing to him by increasing it from twenty pounds to twenty-one pounds. Hence by taking an even chance of winning or losing a sovereign we are, according to Spencer, taking a greater risk of pain than is balanced by the chance of pleasure.

The fallacy resides in this : that the problem is not of a logical but of a psychological character. Although for a man without feelings and wholly logical the pound won is of less value than the pound lost, yet, human nature being as it is. the satisfaction of winning one pound is in fact greater than the pain of losing one pound. Unpleasant thoughts of loss are quickly extruded from the mind, and leave only passing effect, while pleasant thoughts of gain last longer. If the question is to be reduced to one of material satisfaction, Spencer's argument fails for the same reason that some of his philosophy fails—namely, that it is founded on deduction from a principle instead of upon observation. But Spencer argued against gambling on yet another ground : it was wrong, he said, to obtain satisfaction at the cost of another person's dissatisfaction ; it seared the sympathies.

Yet here again it has to be replied that in
moderation and among friends it certainly does
nothing of the kind, but rather the opposite. His
objection to taking money by gambling, on the
ground that it involves pain to another, is analogous to his dislike of Stevenson's " Travels with
a Donkey in the Cevennes," owing to the pain
which he experienced on reading of the donkey
being flogged. In both cases the truth is that he
was trying to justify his puritanical prejudices
by an altogether Quixotic extension of philosophical principles. Spencer could never have
admitted to himself so inconsistent a thing as a
prejudice. His whole thought had to be consistent
with principle. Yet we all have our prejudices ;
and the greatest philosopher will be he who
recognises that they *are* prejudices ; and that it is
better to suffer them gladly than to pervert them
into conformity with principle. As Emerson has
said, " consistency is the essence of absurdity."
A true philosopher must often have occasion to
say : *Video meliora proboque ; deteriora sequor.*
But such a maxim would have been intolerably
offensive to Spencer ; yet he could only escape it
by harbouring perverted views.

As to his other amusements, he is said to have
been fond of skating. He was exceedingly fond of
fishing, and succeeded after some years' absten-
tion in squaring that pursuit with his conscientious

objection to giving pain. The fine arts he did not really appreciate, except in the case of music, to which he was very strongly addicted. Of all the fine arts, music is that which requires the least amount of trained intellectual discernment. For that reason it has usually been the most favoured among those whose intellects, by strong concentration on science and philosophy, have become ill-adapted for moving on æsthetic lines. As regards literature, he can have had little appreciation of style for its own sake. He took no interest at all in biography or history, but, curiously enough, was exceedingly fond of novels. Probably he very seldom in his life read any book from cover to cover, except novels.

The foregoing delineation of Spencer's character has reference chiefly to the most active part of his life. For there is no doubt that he changed considerably as he grew older; and as the great majority of his still-living acquaintances knew him best as an old man, wrong ideas have very readily gained currency. Though still retaining his peculiar gifts, his mind lost its plasticity, and, like his style, appeared to become sclerotic. It very commonly happens among men that those who have retained throughout life and with little modification the convictions of their university days become hardened into one rigid mould of thought. They do not defend their views with

any less energy than before ; but their vivacity is
less the produce of heart and soul than of profound
dogma. The normal progress of years brings perhaps
more usually a wider and more tolerant outlook
upon the world. The old beliefs are still entertained, but with a growing consciousness that there
are other things besides. Spencer, and many like
him, showed no such consciousness : unable to yield
anything of his earlier convictions, those convictions
could only be preserved in their original intensity
as dogmas. The condition of Spencer's health no
doubt accounted for much of what was really a
form of degeneration. His excessive sensitiveness,
his overweening pre-occupation with himself, his
long hours of enforced idleness, must inevitably
have corrupted his outlook upon life. The effects
may be seen in the laborious dullness of the
Autobiography. They may be seen in the elaborate precautions which he took to prevent that
work becoming public before his death. Mr.
Williams, of Messrs. Williams and Norgate, who
were Spencer's publishers, has kindly shown me a
letter which Spencer wrote to his father concerning this Autobiography ; and which I am permitted
by the trustees to publish.

" 64, AVENUE ROAD, N.W.,
Oct. 13*th*, 1889.

" DEAR MR. WILLIAMS,

" As you have taken so much trouble in fulfilling my
wishes with respect to the printing of the Autobiography,

I feel that it is but a small return on my part to give you the option of being one among the first half-dozen to whom the volume is lent. In all preliminary letters to friends I am including the following paragraphs.

" ' I had originally intended to print fifty presentation copies for friends, but consideration made it manifest that were so large a number distributed and permanently left with those to whom they were sent, not a very long time would elapse before a copy would find its way to America, since in many cases copies would be lent and not very carefully looked after by the loanees. Publication there would not only defeat my intention to withhold the book from the public during my life, but would entail loss of the English copyright. A comparatively safe course seemed to be that of printing half a dozen copies for the purpose of lending to friends for short periods ; and this has been the course taken.

" ' There still remains, however, a certain amount of risk ; since, when known in America, as it will presently be, that some copies are in circulation, efforts will be made by piratical publishers to obtain one through the agency of servants or others. Hence the need for precautions. Any friend to whom the volume is lent must promise that while in his or her possession it shall not be allowed to leave the house ; that while in the house it shall not be seen by anyone connected with the press, or who might be likely to make any public use of its contents ; and that when not in hand it shall be kept under lock and key. Doubtless the risk in each case is very small ; but just as one insures against fire, not with the expectation that the house will be burnt down, but to be secure against the very remote risk of its being burnt down, so these precautions are to be taken, not against the *probability* of escape, but against the *possibility* of escape.

" ' The volume should be returned in ten days or sooner,

and as a security let me request that, when sent back by post, it may be registered.'

" I am, truly yours,

"HERBERT SPENCER."

Spencer's will was characteristically individualist. The first clause directed that he should be cremated without any form of religious ceremony, after being placed in a coffin "with a loose lid easily opened from below." Various small bequests were made to a number of people ; but the bulk of his property was placed in trust for the continuance of "The Descriptive Sociology." Mr. Auberon Herbert, Dr. Charlton Bastian, and Dr. David Duncan were appointed trustees, and Mr. Henry Tedder the first secretary to the trust. Apart from the bequests above alluded to, the income derived from the sale of his works, as well as from investments, was to be spent in bringing out new volumes of "The Descriptive Sociology " dealing with peoples not previously dealt with, and in republishing parts both of the old and new volumes in a more handy form. When this work was concluded the whole of Spencer's estate was to be sold, and the proceeds divided between twelve scientific societies which he named (but which did not include the Royal Society), on the understanding that the money should be spent by them within five years of its receipt, and not used for any purposes of endowment. At the present moment, two new volumes of " The Descriptive Sociology " have appeared since Spencer's death ; and Dr. Duncan is the only surviving trustee.

Judgments on Spencer's character are likely to vary with the critic. We shall perhaps be well-advised to refrain from judging at all. He may have had many qualities which we do not care for ; but he had many others which placed him morally as well as intellectually high above the average man. It is a vice of the present age to insist that a man shall come up to a certain all-round standard in mental and moral qualities. If he falls in certain respects below that standard, it is held insufficient that he should soar high above it in other respects. As our social policy has drifted for long in the direction of dead-level equality, so there is a constant tendency, in judging men, to require a certain general conformity in all directions before we feel free to admire qualities of the highest rarity and excellence. Yet this attitude is irrational ; for the excessive development of a few mental faculties almost inevitably carries under-development of others. In proportion as we require conformity to the prevailing standard, and in proportion as that standard is high and far reaching, we cut away the basis of greatness and of genius. If we judge great men by their foibles we condemn our own common sense. Surely

we must allow some latitude to genius : we must
regard the aberrations of genius with a more tolerant
eye than the aberrations of commonplace people.
Spencer had astonishing intellectual powers ; he
summed up the thought and spirit of his time as
no other writer could have done : the whole of
modern thought is founded, consciously or unconsciously, on Spencer's work. Many seem to regard
him wholly from the point of view of the weaknesses inherent in a great character ; but these
charges merely recoil on the head of those who
make them and who are ready to judge a man,
not by what he did in the world, but by the least
relevant of his deficiencies. I feel indeed some
sadness in the thought that any such observations
should appear to be called for. If we are going to
judge great men by reference to the narrow ambit
of our personal sentiments, what hope shall there
be for genius in the future ? If society is to produce great men, the atmosphere must be tolerant
and free.

CHAPTER IV

THE Synthetic Philosophy is divided into two parts of very unequal length. Part i., "The Unknowable," occupies little more than the first hundred pages of "First Principles." Part ii., "The Knowable," occupies all the remainder of the work : that is to say, by far the larger part of "First Principles," and the whole of the nine succeeding volumes. The Philosophy, in so far as it concerns "The Knowable," has five main divisions. The first of these is "First Principles," in which are laid down the main philosophic doctrines, which are applied to the various special departments of knowledge in the subsequent divisions. We begin with "The Principles of Biology," then "The Principles of Psychology," then "The Principles of Sociology," and finally "The Principles of Ethics," which Spencer regarded as the flower of the Philosophy, and the goal to which all the preceding volumes led.

In addition to these ten volumes Spencer published eight other volumes, which may be regarded as subsidiary to the main philosophical work. Most important of these is "The Study of

Sociology," which was intended to be preparatory
to his formal sociological treatises.   There are
three volumes of long essays, and two smaller
volumes of short essays : the former mainly written
when he was young, and marking the stages in
the growth of his system of thought ; the latter
written when he was old, and touching in a more
casual way on a great variety of topics which
happened to interest him for the moment.   Then
there is his first book " Social Statics," the revised
edition of which is now bound up with four articles
reprinted from the *Contemporary Review* under the
title of " The Man *versus* the State."   His work
on " Education " will be described later ;   and
finally there are the two volumes of Autobiography.

Before descending into the details of this
immense system of thought, it will be well to take
a bird's-eye view over the whole.   Spencer was
a man whose theories and conduct in life were all
subordinated to and explained by a small number
of general principles.   Anyone turning over at
hazard the pages of one of the philosophical
volumes would be overwhelmed by the multitude
of facts and details brought forward.   He would
be lost as to the meaning of it all : he could not see
the wood for the trees.   But when once the very
few principles at the basis of Spencer's mind are
understood, the rest becomes easy.   Every principle drew to itself like a magnet all the facts

from every department of knowledge which in any way illustrated or supported it; and the *meaning* of this maze of detail at once becomes clear.

There are two fundamental ideas at the root of the Philosophy. The first is that of universal evolution; the second is the guiding principle of his social and political writings. As regards the doctrine of evolution, Spencer early in life rejected the supposition that the universe was a thing created and stationary. He perceived that all Nature was in a constant state of change or flux; and he endeavoured to find some law which should describe the tendencies of such change— a law which should be equally applicable to the change of a nebula into a star or stellar system, and of a protozoan animal into a man. This law he called the law of Evolution. It proposed to describe the various stages characteristic of all progress in all departments of Nature as the universe grows older. He believed that the outlines of such changes were similar throughout all varieties of the changing substance.

The second fundamental conception of the Philosophy, and perhaps the more important, as it was certainly the larger section, is devoted to political and social thought. When Spencer was a very young man he found himself in the midst of what were then very Radical surroundings.

His father was almost, if not quite, a Quaker;
his uncle, Thomas Spencer, was an advanced
reformer and forerunner of the school of Man-
chester Radicals. Spencer himself was of an
insubordinate mind, to which restrictions of any
kind were insupportable. Can it be wondered at
that he eagerly caught up the catchword of
Liberty and proceeded to identify social progress
with the admission of every individual to the
maximum freedom consistent with social order
and security? When very young he went even
beyond the latter condition. He accepted the
Quaker view that all war was wrong; and that
the maintenance of military forces was no part
of the duties of the State, but on the other hand
to be condemned as an infringement of individual
freedom. But he soon saw the visionary nature
of such an ideal: he soon admitted that the
defence of the State from foreign aggression was
as much a part of the duties of government as the
protection of individuals at home from the aggression of criminals. Yet throughout his life he
preserved an inveterate hatred of war and of
militarism. Peace was the first fundamental corollary from his doctrine of liberty.

The second corollary proposed to limit the
functions of government to the single sphere of
police duty. Any further coercion of the individual by the State he regarded as an improper

encroachment on individual liberty. To take the extreme cases, he condemned the control of sanitary administration or the upkeep of roads by the State : such work fell to private corporations of citizens who undertook it as a matter of ordinary business, and who, of course, had no coercive power over their fellows, except by the exclusion of those who refused to pay, from the advantages offered them. He objected to the Post Office being in the hands of the State, and still more to its being a monopoly. And he óbjected to State education, first on the grounds of its compulsory character, and secondly because the Government had no right to tax citizens for a purpose which, even if beneficial, was not part of their natural duties. Extreme though these views now appear, it must be remembered that they did not seem nearly so extreme then. Moreover, it is unwise to condemn a general principle because its applications have been pushed too far ; but to this subsequent reference will be made.

In any case, Evolution and Liberty are the two guiding stars of Spencer's philosophy. Evolution professes to be a statement of fact ; it records the direction in which the material and spiritual changes of the universe are tending. Liberty, on the other hand, is put forward as a human aim and the highest injunction of political ethics. It is natural that, as we shall see, he should endeavour to connect the two. But all that here remains to be said is that when once the reader has grasped these fundamental conceptions of Spencer's mind he has already advanced a long way towards the comprehension of the System of Philosophy.

Doubtless Spencer had numerous lesser principles, but none which dominated his work to anything like the same extent. To all these lesser principles reference will be made in due course. His biology contains several doctrines of importance, not connected either with evolution or with liberty. Moreover, he had a special metaphysical doctrine of his own. The average reader would perhaps be surprised to find that Spencer's Philosophy scarcely touches at all on metaphysics. With the exception of a short part of " First Principles " and of " The Principles of Psychology," there is no metaphysics in his Philosophy, and even these small portions are extraneous and unnecessary to the main argument. The bulk of the Philosophy is devoted to problems of science, not metaphysics : for even the law of general evolution, though not belonging to any one branch of science, belongs in a sense to all, and is based, like all science, wholly on the observation of material facts.

Such being the general plan of the Philosophy, let us pass now to consider its method. All additions to knowledge, except in the case of metaphysics (which many regard as not being knowledge), are based in the last resort upon observation of natural phenomena. But the mere accumulation of facts does not constitute knowledge : the facts have to be co-ordinated; generalisations have to be made : the facts have to be united or strung together on a general principle—laws, that is to say, have to be formulated, which endow the facts with meaning and value, in the human sense. And these laws may be attained by one of the two opposite methods of induction or deduction. In induction we start with the accumulation of facts, and by probing about among them, looking for similarities and dissimilarities, we form *theories* and learn how they are connected together. In deduction, on the other hand, we *start* with the theory. It may be derived either from inductions reached elsewhere, or it may be a hypothesis invented by our own minds. At any rate, we start with a theory and then proceed to the accumulation of facts to see how the theory fits them. If it does not fit them (as commonly happens at the first trials), we discard it or modify it until it does fit them. But unfortunately the *amour-propre* of humanity does not easily discard its pet theories ; and it frequently happens that instead of the theory being discarded the facts are twisted about and arranged in such a way as apparently to be covered by it. It is from the universal tendency towards such illegitimate manipulation that the deductive method has fallen into such deep discredit in many branches of science.

Now the whole of Spencer's Philosophy was worked out by the deductive method. It is probable that he would have objected to so sweeping a statement; but nevertheless it is true. It is probable that he would have pointed to the tables of " The Descriptive Sociology " as evidence of his inductive procedure. " The Descriptive Sociology " consists of a vast accumulation of facts of all kinds that could be of any use in the formation of sociological theories. The facts were collected from immense numbers of books of travel, and of description of native races; they were mainly selected by private secretaries who had no special theory in view, but cut out from the books they read *any* fact which in their opinion had *any* significance with regard to *any* sociological theory whatever. It is necessary also to admit that Spencer accumulated these facts, at great expense to himself, *before* writing his " Principles of Sociology," and for the professed purpose of supplying himself with a basis for that work. Here, then, would appear to be a plain instance of the inductive method. Great piles of facts first accumulated from completely impartial sources: a careful study of those facts; and then three volumes of " Sociology" containing the principles generalised from them.

But the appearance of induction is only an appearance. The solid truth remains that Spencer's fundamental theories were formed long in advance of the compilation of " The Descriptive Sociology." I do not mean to deny that many of the minor theories of the " Sociology" may have been derived by true induction ; but the major theories—the necessity for peace and for the limitation of Government functions—were entertained by Spencer long before he ever heard of or knew the meaning of, the word " sociology " ; and the net result of " The Principles of Sociology " is to establish, with the greatest abundance of evidence and at the greatest length, just those very doctrines which Spencer had so warmly espoused in early manhood. It may perhaps be replied that it is hard if he should be debarred from the inductive method merely on the ground that he previously held true theories : it may be urged that the theories of the " Sociology " were based on induction, whether or not he happened to hold them before. All that is true ; but the outstanding fact remains that the two great doctrines of his " Sociology" and " Ethics " are just the two doctrines which he imbibed with the greatest avidity in his early years as a political agitator. It would indeed be a fortunate coinci-

dence if a young man, without knowledge and
without study, were to hit by chance on the two
social principles which subsequent research showed
to be the fundamental conditions of social welfare.
It would be still more strange if the enthusiastic
advocacy of those principles, before they had any
basis of knowledge, should bear so intimate a
resemblance to the equally enthusiastic advocacy
of them after they had been independently established on a basis of observation and induction.
Indeed, it cannot be seriously denied that, in the
main, Spencer formed his theories *first*, and
established them by induction *afterwards*.

Nor is the case different with the other great
principle of the Philosophy—the law of universal
evolution. This theory grew out of a statement
which he read in von Baer—to the effect that the
embryonic development of animals is always from
the homogeneous to the heterogeneous. Here was
a theory such as Spencer's mind delighted in : it
stuck fast in his memory when all the other details
of von Baer had faded away. It obsessed him ;
he went about applying it all round ; every kind
of change around him presented itself as a progress
from homogeneity to heterogeneity : this mode of
development appeared to be illustrated in every
class of natural phenomenon. Gradually the law
grew. Development was not only from the homogeneous to the heterogeneous : it was from the

simple to the complex; from the incoherent to the coherent; from the indefinite to the definite, and so on. Spencer was a mono-ideist; the same idea revolved incessantly in his brain, gathering to itself every sort of cognate doctrine, until at last it seemed to fill the whole universe. And here again it must be remarked what a fortunate coincidence it was that a raw and unlearned youth should have seized by chance the one doctrine which his subsequent research showed to be the fundamental law of universal change. The marvel is that his immature opinions should so very rarely have failed to be supported and established by subsequent induction.

An even more striking instance of this mode of procedure is found in his doctrine of Organic Evolution. It was necessary to his theory that animals and plants should all have evolved from the most elementary unicellular organisms. Accordingly he was an ardent believer in Organic Evolution years before Darwin and Wallace enunciated their theory of Natural Selection. In 1852 he wrote an article in order to show that Organic Evolution had arisen from the unique factor of the inheritance of acquired characters, for he could not think of any other factor. Here he was entirely mistaken. Writing now at a distance of much more than half a century from this essay —a half-century filled with the most intense biological speculation and spirit of inquiry—it may be stated that not one single fact has come to light which justifies the belief that acquired characters are inherited. Yet Spencer was prepared to base the whole theory of evolution on the assumption that every individual item of progress has arisen from that single and unaided factor. Of course, when Natural Selection was discovered he modified his views. But the fact remains that so long as his theory required the assistance of a spurious factor, so long did he consider that factor quite adequate to support it.

The truth is that Spencer had the makings of a fanatic, and herein lie both his strength and his weakness. The stream of thought in a fanatic is a narrow one. Nothing counts outside the province on which attention is concentrated. But within that province the waters flow with irresistible violence between their narrow banks and carry every obstacle before them. Simeon Stylites could never have stood upon a pillar for forty years if his mind had been free to pass the limitations of a single obsessing idea. Spencer also had his few groundwork principles; and so strongly did they move him that he, naturally an idle man, was driven to erect the most voluminous and elaborate system of thought of his time.

But it may be observed that at all events the

theory of evolution was true. Spencer conceived
the right principle, although he supported it on
wrong grounds. And so, too, it may be inferred
that perhaps, after all, much of his social teaching
was correct. The views he put forward were
indeed representative of the best and most advanced political thought in the country at the
time when he was young. May it not be, then,
that he was a man of very strong natural pene-
tration, and that his prepossessions, however
violent, were founded on a true instinct? Such
indeed was most probably the case, and such is
the thesis that will subsequently be developed.
But it is best to clear the ground at the outset by
admitting that they *were* prepossessions.

Spencer's mind moving among facts was like
a magnet moving among metal filings. If we
throw together a medley of filings of iron, silver,
nickel, and tin, and then pass a magnet over the
heap, the iron filings will rise forth and cluster
round the magnet, while the other metals will lie
still. If the experiment is performed carefully,
the heap will soon be deprived of *all* its iron, while
no particle of the silver, nickel, or tin will have
been removed. And so it happened when Spencer
applied his sociological principles to the accumulation of facts in " The Descriptive Sociology."
Every fact which illuminated those principles was
drawn out and clustered round the magnet, while

the remaining facts lay unseen and untouched. For this reason Spencer's Philosophy *does* present a vast agglomeration of facts—the appearance of an encyclopædic knowledge and of genuine induction. But for this reason also it was possible to say of him, " Scratch Spencer, and you find ignorance." The residue of facts not affected by his magnets remained to him a sealed and unknown book. And be it added, without his magnets he would have known nothing : he had not the spirit of the observer, who can amass isolated facts and slowly evolve a theory to connect them. There was no room for an isolated fact in his mind ; it would drop out at once. Yet it speaks much for the all-embracing character of his principles that they could draw to themselves so many verifying circumstances. Considering his methods, the gaps were wonderfully few. The question is to what extent they are vital to his theories.

That Spencer would have admitted this *modus operandi* is scarcely probable. Even Newton understood his own methods so little as to say *hypotheses non fingo*. But the whole scheme of Spencer's Philosophy bears the traces of its method. Each separate work bears the title " Principles " ; it was in principles alone that he was interested. And the entire Philosophy is entitled " Synthetic," meaning a bringing together or clustering of phenomena around a single focus or principle or law, or, as by previous analogy, magnet. His great aim was the unification of knowledge : the discovery of a single formula which should unite all classes of phenomena in the universe ; a magnet which would attract every variety of metal in any heap and leave no residue at all.

With this general view of the aim and methods of Spencer's Philosophy we may now proceed to consider it in detail. It will be my purpose not only to furnish an account of the outlines of his system of thought, but to indicate the attitude of modern knowledge with regard to it.

CHAPTER V

A HUNDRED years ago civilised societies were commonly classified into those which were mainly democratic, those which were oligarchical, and those which were monarchical. Of the two latter types there was already considerable knowledge ; the advanced thinkers of the time tended very generally to condemn them and to fix their hopes for the regeneration of the world on the triumphant establishment of democracy. The course of political action followed, as usually happens, the course of philosophical speculation ; and throughout the nineteenth century a gradual progress of democratic institutions was witnessed in all the civilised countries of the world.

It soon became apparent, however, that whatever benefits might be derived from democracy, it certainly was not the general panacea for all social evils that its early enthusiasts had hoped. Undoubtedly the nineteenth century was marked by an immense increase of knowledge and of material prosperity in all ranks of society. But these improvements were due in large part to the huge increase of wealth following on the development of railways, the universal introduction of machinery, and the consequent expansion of trade. It is not to be denied that improved methods of government did contribute to some extent to the new social prosperity; but for the first three-quarters of the century democratic legislation was directed mainly towards the breaking up of the remnants of feudalism rather than to the introduction of definite schemes of constructive improvement. At all events, philosophers began to doubt the all-embracing efficacy of democratic ideals, in proportion as those ideals began to sink into the minds of the people at large. In this predicament some new dividing line between societies was sought—some classification based upon a deeper analysis than that of democracies and monarchies. The practical experiments of France in various types of government furnished much material for generalisation; for that country of advanced thought oscillated between a republic and a monarchy, without any great differences being effected in the lives or social conditions of the people. The most profound alterations in the *form* of government appeared to carry no corresponding alterations in the real prosperity of the community. It was clearly necessary to draw some more fundamental line between types of government than that suggested by a merely superficial glance.

The new analysis of social types found its most perfect expression in the works of Herbert Spencer. He preached the doctrine that the two fundamental types of society are those in which there is much government, and those in which there is little government. All classes of political thinkers of course recognise the necessity for *some* government, even if limited to the preservation of internal order and the defence against foreign aggression. But beyond this minimum or common basis government may ramify deeply into all branches of society and affect the lives of citizens at almost every turn, whether by restrictions or commands, and with the associated burden of a heavy taxation ; or on the other hand, it may hold aloof and leave citizens to live their own lives with scarcely any interference, save such as are plainly indispensable, and demanding only a small taxation, to meet the cost of the few functions undertaken. This distinction was adopted by Spencer as the basis of a true classification of societies. The division into democracies, oligarchies, etc., he regarded as concerned only with the *form* of government ; the new division concerned the *substance* of government, and was therefore a far more important and fundamental classification. Changes in the form of government such as those which took place last century in France do not affect the lives of the people, because the substance of government remains unchanged throughout.

Having established the distinction between the two main types of society, Spencer proceeds to ascertain the characteristics exhibited by each. He finds that the type which exhibits much government generally prevails where wars are common; while the type which exhibits little government is specially associated with peace. Where the safety of the community is in jeopardy from external enemies, it is clearly necessary that the activities of individuals should be subordinated to the needs of the State : society has to be organised on a military basis. Where, on the other hand, wars are rare, social development proceeds along industrial lines. In commerce and industry men are more likely to put forth their best efforts when working for their own welfare than when working for the welfare of the State. Hence industrial and individual freedom characterises those societies which are the least addicted to war. The two fundamental types of society are thus named, according to their principal characteristics, the military and industrial types—the former showing much and the latter little control of individual activities by the State.

The military type of society is again divisible into two other classes—namely, the purely military type organised for the purposes of war, and

the socialistic type organised for the supposed
welfare of its citizens. It might appear at first
sight that socialistic and military societies are
antithetical. This Spencer denies, for both are
characterised by an extensive governmental organisation limiting and directing the activities of
citizens. The circumstance that the organisation is established for different aims does not
obscure the fact that the organisation exists, nor
can it conceal the fundamental similarity between
the two kinds. In evidence of this proposition
Spencer points out the close association between
Militarism and Socialism in modern European
countries. The most extreme form of despotism
is found in Russia, and there too occur the most
violent forms of Socialism and anarchy. Germany
is one of the most military nations of Europe ; and
it has a larger proportion of Socialists than any
other country. On the other hand, England is the
least military of European nations, being until
lately the only one which did not have conscription. And the Socialist propaganda in England
is likewise the weakest in Europe. All this which
was true last century still remains true. The
growing military organisations of foreign countries
have been accompanied by a rapid progress
of socialistic legislation. And in England—the
nearest approach to the pure industrial type—
military and socialistic ideals have grown hand

in hand. Our Government at the outbreak of the present war had gone farther in the direction of Socialism than any previous Government in our history. Yet within a few weeks, and with scarcely a change of *personnel*, it embarked upon military operations likewise without a parallel through all our great wars in the past. Where the people are accustomed to Government control, where there exist normally large regulative organisations, those organisations can without excessive dislocation be employed for meeting new needs suddenly arisen.

Spencer gave some attention to the relation between the form and substance of Government. A democracy differs from a monarchy only in form; in the one case a king rules, in the other case a majority of the people rules : in each case the individual may be more or less free, or more or less under Government control. In an essay on " Representative Government " published in 1857, he reached the conclusion that democratic forms are the best of all others for the purely industrial type of society; but that for the military type of society it is the worst of all others. Where the sphere of Government is large, democracies cannot pay attention to the workings of its numerous ramifications. Moreover, mobs are the most dangerous of tyrants. From a dictator there is always an ultimate appeal to the people; his conduct is controlled by what the people will tolerate. But from a majority of the people there is no appeal. The tyranny of a majority is subject to no limitations. When, however, it is clearly understood that the functions of Government may not pass certain limits, then representative institutions constitute the best form of government. Tyranny is impossible, when the expansion of government is prevented. In another essay Spencer urges that interests, and not persons, should be represented. The labouring classes under universal suffrage would possess far more political power than they were entitled to ; and other interests, not less important to the State, would be prejudiced and overwhelmed by an unfair majority.

These are the main doctrines of Spencer's purely sociological works, namely " Descriptive Sociology " and " The Principles of Sociology." The former work is a compilation in folio volumes, in which the leading traits of different societies are exhibited in tabular form. Their purpose is to ascertain what kinds of social institutions commonly go together, the relation, for instance, between militancy and trade or domestic institutions, the *status* of women, etc. The generalisations thus obtained form the body of " The Principles of Sociology." Its main results are the establishment, as already stated, of two chief types of society, and a description of the general characteristics of each. Spencer finds that the industrial type is distinguished by most of the virtues, and the military type by most of the vices. A high *status* of women and children, a strong philanthropy, a vigorous initiative and disregard of authority, a strong and sympathetic character, go with the industrial type, in addition to its main feature of great individual freedom. But cruelty, revenge, superstition, and brutality go with the militant type, offset only by the virtues of obedience, patriotism, and loyalty to rulers. That other loyalty, consisting in a high standard of truthfulness and hatred of fraud or deception, is conspicuously lacking in militant societies, and conspicuously present in industrial societies. Of all these doctrines, a complete account will be found in the following chapter.

In all scientific investigations the truth is generally reached by a gradual elimination of error. Spencer plainly thought that he had reached a final settlement of the proper classification of societies. Such a result was indeed very unlikely to be achieved the moment the science of sociology was founded : zoology had been in existence for centuries before anything approaching a true classification of animals had been discovered ; one scheme of classification was discarded after another, each one being on the whole a nearer

approximation to the truth than its predecessor.
So, too, in sociology, the features which constitute
the really fundamental points of difference between
societies are scarcely likely to be isolated till
after laborious research lasting over generations.
A general principle, such as that laid down by
Spencer, falls to the ground if *one fact* can be
named with which it is incompatible. It appears
that the modern industrial development of Germany constitutes just such a fact. According to
Spencer, the militant and industrial *régimes* are
antagonistic: a rapid industrial development
carries with it an immense increase of individual
liberty and a reduction in the functions of the
State. Yet in Germany the industrial development has gone with a corresponding military
development, and with an extension of State functions. Indeed, it seems to some extent to have
been due to the initiative and enterprise of the
State, which according to Spencer could only
have acted as a drag by the imposition of burden-
some restrictions.

Nevertheless Spencer probably arrived at a
truer notion of sociology than existed before
him. Between nations organised for war and
nations organised for peace there does exist a
more fundamental difference than between a
monarchy and a republic, as such. There is
far more real community between the English

monarchy and the French or American republics than there is between the English and Russian monarchies. The amount of interference by Government with individual liberty is a true criterion of the condition of society ; but it is not the whole truth ; it is only an adumbration of the truth. Spencer's sociology was unfortunately under the immediate and powerful bias of his Ethics. From the earliest days, he was strongly inclined to peace, a hater of militarism, and a believer in individual liberty. Societies which exhibited these traits naturally appeared to him to stand out in a separate class, to which the militant type, so repugnant to him, was the antithesis. But the fundamental antagonism between the two was perhaps as much a reflection of Spencer's mind as of objective facts. It is possible to go even farther. At the time when he was developing his theories, about the middle of last century, there *was* a real antithesis between militarism and industrialism : the activities of the State *were* aimed to some extent against an industrial *régime ;* and at that time there was considerable truth in the doctrine that the development of industry implied the abolition of restrictions by the State. But Spencer had no historical sense ; he seems to have inferred that because Government activities were injurious then, they must always be so in any sphere whatever. Accordingly he was led to

condemn the introduction of national education ;
and also all forms of sanitary supervision by the
Government. In very early youth he even denied
the right of the Government to maintain an army
or navy ; but this extreme doctrine was soon
struck out from among his beliefs ; it was expressed
only in the first edition of " Social Statics," which
for half a century has been out of print. In all
his later writings he emphasised the somewhat
obvious truth that the national defence is the
prime duty of Government ; and he even admitted
that in times of public danger through war the
Government has an absolute right over the lives
and properties of all its citizens.

As regards national education, most readers
will doubtless regard Spencer's views with a smile
of contemptuous superiority. Yet it is certainly
the case that all Spencer's prophecies on this subject have turned out to be far more accurate than
those of the reformers who initiated it. It was
generally believed that universal education would
finally abolish all the evils of social life. Immense
things were expected of it, not one-tenth part of
which have been realised. The sanguine tempera-
ment of mankind is always ready to believe in a
high-sounding remedy, which will lift humanity
out of its vulgar barbarism into a race of super-
men. Inventors may know that not one in a
thousand of the inventions that are patented ever

achieve success ; but inventions continue to be patented in undiminished number. Authors may know that not one in a hundred of the books that are written ever find a publisher ; yet books continue to be written in the inexpugnable hope that large profits may accrue from them. The columns of our newspapers are filled with advertisements of patent medicines, for which the most absurd and extravagant claims are made. Yet year after year humanity squanders huge sums in the purchase of these drugs, of which some are injurious, most are useless, and nearly all vastly inferior to the remedies publicly recognised by the science of medicine.

If men are thus irrationally sanguine in the simpler matters of life, it is natural they should be still more so in the complex affairs of social government, where the guidance of experience is less available. The people who advocated national education thought that it would be the forerunner of permanent peace ; for as people knew more and became more refined they would naturally be less addicted to war. The belief like so many *à priori* convictions, seemed eminently reasonable ; and the reformers would have utterly declined to believe that, after half a century of compulsory education throughout Europe, the inhabitants of that continent would have embarked upon the bloodiest war in all history, and a war in which a

larger proportion of the people rushed to engage
than in any previous period known to history,
with the possible exception of the first crusade.
The reformers figured to themselves an enlightened
public reading useful and edifying works : they
did not anticipate that universal reading would
call into existence an enormous flood of villainous
literature and journalism, by which for a few
halfpennies the people would be enabled to
debauch their minds to the lowest pit of degradation. By arguments such as these did Spencer
attempt to defend his views. Nor can they be
dismissed with the contempt that it has long been
fashionable to pour upon them. For what was the
alternative ? If there had been no compulsory
education, the bulk of the people would still have
been educated in private schools. Only the surplus of the population would have remained unable
to read or write ; and there are only too many
occupations where reading and writing are unnecessary. The immense taxation on account of
education would have been non-existent, and the
money so saved would have gone to stimulate
industry and added to the capital of the country.
But all this is part of the larger question which
must now be considered.

Most of the ideals for social reform fall under
the motto of the French Revolution—*Liberté,
Egalité, Fraternité.* Of *Fraternité* there is not

much to be said ; few can question the desirability of attaining it, and even fewer will imagine that it may be established by law. But of *Liberté* and *Egalité* there is much to be said ; for the conviction has gradually been growing that these high sounding titles embody ideals which are irreconcilable. The natural inequality of men is such that it can only be abolished by deep inroads on individual liberty ; and social freedom similarly results in a rapid inequality of social *status*. We are within certain limits obliged to choose between the two, recognising that we are unable to have both. For the last few decades the notion of equality has been the inspiration of nearly all social legislation. It is felt that those who are poor are no worse, and are often better, than those who are rich ; and there appears to be a grave injustice in the present social system which offers all the advantages and opportunities in life to a few while withholding them from the many, without the smallest reference to personal merit. In a wealthy community like our own this sentiment does not issue in sudden revolutions, directed towards the hopeless aim of an immediate reconstitution of society. But it does get expressed by the general drift of legislation towards the establishment of greater equality : we have not set up Socialism and Equality, but each of our new Acts of Parliament carries us a step further

in that direction, and is inspired by an ideal
unconsciously felt rather than consciously thought.
The most specious cry of Socialism is "equality
of opportunity." It is recognised by most people
in their calmer moments that men cannot all be
equal. But the plausible argument is advanced
that all should have equal opportunities of securing
the favoured positions in our social system.

Now it is an inherent misfortune of those who
attack the ideal of equality to be associated with
the Conservative school, who may be said to be
biassed in favour of the maintenance of that
particular social system in which they and their
families are pre-eminent. It is possible, however,
to take a purely scientific view of the whole thing ;
and Spencer—an ideal Radical—cannot be accused
by anyone who has the least knowledge of him
of any sort of merely conservative taint. The
question for him all pivoted on liberty. It was
pointed out by Lord Bryce some years ago that,
whereas the leaders of thought last century were
inclined to favour the Liberal party, they are in
the present century inclined to favour the Conservative. The true inwardness of this indubitable
fact is that they are on the whole biassed in favour
of freedom, which was the watchword of the
Liberal party last century, and that they are on
the whole biassed against equality, which is the
watchword of the Liberal party in the present

century. Two highly distinguished and non-political men of science stand out now with especial prominence in opposition to the cry of equality; the one Dr. F. W. Mott, F.R.S., and the other Professor William Bateson, F.R.S., who regarded the matter as of such first-rate importance that he dealt with it in his Presidential Address to the British Association in 1914. It is still, as it always has been, one of the most fundamental issues of social ethics; and under one form or other is certain to come forward again immediately the present hostilities are concluded.

It is a paradox of Socialism to think wholly in terms of individuals. The ultimate sentiment of Socialists is the feeling of injustice aroused by an arrangement under which the goods of the world are held by a few, who are no better than those condemned to comparative poverty. Yet the problem is not of individuals, but of what is best for society as a whole, and of what leads to the greatest happiness on the average of *all* the individuals who make up society. And before passing on to the positive arguments against equality, two facts may be noted which already go far towards destroying the arguments in favour of equality. The first of these is the profound psychological truth that wealth is not the source of happiness; and if we want to raise the sum-total of happiness, we are travelling along altogether

the wrong road if we think to achieve it by an
equal distribution of wealth. That indeed is a
gross form of ethical materialism, and as far
removed as can be from any true insight into
human character. Is the *rentier* a happier man
than the *employé* ? Is the millionaire happier than
the factory girl ? Few who know both classes will
answer these questions in the affirmative ; for
human nature has not changed since the eighth
century, when Abdalrahman, the monarch of
Cordova, whose magnificence is famous, exclaimed :

" I have now reigned above fifty years in victory or
peace; beloved by my subjects, dreaded by my enemies,
and respected by my allies. Riches and honours, power
and pleasure, have waited on my call, nor does any earthly
blessing appear to have been wanting to my felicity. In
this situation I have diligently numbered the days of pure
and genuine happiness which have fallen to my lot : they
amount to Fourteen : O man, place not thy confidence
in this present world ! " [1]

Once again, in the twentieth century the
accumulation of wealth among *all* classes is far
greater than ever before in our history. Are we
then to infer that men are happier now than ever
before ? and that in all the centuries of our history
no such happiness has been known as that which
we now experience ? Surely not. Two qualifications indeed have to be made. First, a poverty
which cuts off the *real* necessaries of life does bring

[1] Gibbon, vi., 26.

unhappiness ; and, secondly, a poverty which cuts off the *artificial* necessaries does the same. The possession of a certain income very quickly generates new wants : the ability to satisfy them soon constitutes them into necessaries ; and the privation of them brings as much real misery as the privation of food to a man who has always been poor. It is impossible to name any sum, such as £400 a year, which brings happiness to all. For a millionaire it would involve privation which would imply complete wretchedness, and often before now has even led to suicide. For an unskilled labourer it would bring at first extravagant joy, until after a few years his new luxuries had become necessities, and he would find himself with as many fresh and unsatisfied wants as he had before. But apart from these qualifications there is no genuine relation between wealth and happiness ; and as a mere scientific fact a more equal distribution of wealth *would not* lead to a general increase of happiness : the means are wrongly contrived for the end in view. Equal distribution may possibly be right on other grounds, but for raising the standard of happiness it is irrelevant.

The second fact to be named with regard to the equality campaign is that it is based on sentiments of the nature of jealousy. There is a real, often unconfessed, feeling of animosity against those

who have much, so often out of proportion to their
deserts.   Ostentation is always bad taste—the
symbol of vanity and a little mind.   But apart
from ostentation, it is inevitable that A. should
speculate why B., no better than himself, should
be so much more kindly endowed by society ;
and from this sentiment, usually not intense, but
strong by reason of its ubiquity, springs perhaps
the main origin of equality legislation.   It is to be
hoped that there is no need to labour the argument
that social reform based on *animosity against*
individuals is necessarily unsound at core.   True
reform must be animated by pure philanthropy,
guided by reason ;   it should be inspired by the
single-minded desire for the benefit of society or
of individuals, never by hostility to individuals
or to any class of them.   If we really desire to
achieve by legislation the welfare of humanity,
there must be no jealousy lurking in our minds :
there must be no suspicion of acting merely out
of hostility to others, or to get square with them.
But it is not easy to realise in practice the pure
spirit of *fraternité* which is so essential to true
political progress.

If many of the arguments used in favour of
equality are unsound, there are various arguments
of an opposite character which furnish cogent
reasons against that ideal.   As already observed,
the matter at issue is not concerned with the wel-

fare of individuals, but with the welfare of society as a whole. And if it is shown that inequality is a wholesome state of society, the outraged sentiments of some individuals must simply be disregarded. From the point of view of society as a whole the position is this : that the work of the world is of very diverse character and requires very diverse kinds of quality and education in those who perform it. Of the necessary work of society, a very large part is unskilled routine or drudgery, needing little beyond continued muscular effort from those to whose lot it falls. Skilled manual labour constitutes another large *desideratum* of social life, though the number of individuals occupied in it is smaller than that devoted to the lower types of duty. The skilled manual labourer does not *need* a large general education. He requires a high development, chiefly muscular, of a single quality. A still smaller class comprise those whose work is mainly mental : they are engaged in the direction and organisation of affairs. The work of this class calls for such qualities as judgment, intelligence, and decision —the development of which implies a much higher degree of general education.

Finally, the progress of the world needs yet another class—of men of science, authors, artists, musicians, etc. This class is more closely associated with the ideals of progress than of order ; it can hardly be described as essential to the orderly continuance of society, yet it takes precedence of all others as being intimately bound up with the state of civilisation. Upon it civilisation depends ; and from it emanate the new discoveries and the new ideals which ultimately stimulate social progress, lead to the happiness and improvement of mankind, and constitute the highest expression of human life, by which our societies of men are differentiated from societies of bees or ants. This class is and should be the smallest of all ; and in general the mental cultivation required for it is of the utmost intensity and rigour—so intense and vigorous indeed as often to involve (as in Spencer's case) a permanently enfeebled physical constitution.

Such in very rough outline is the work that society has to do. We may visualise a community of civilised men in the form of a pyramid, the base of which is constituted by the dull and stupid labour of physical existence, and demanding the largest single class of individuals. As we ascend the pyramid the work is of progressively higher type and the class devoted to it becomes progressively smaller ; till, near the apex, the work is one of the highest virtuosity and the number of workers is exceedingly small. It is clear already that inequality is of the essence of healthy social life. Those near the apex would be plunged in hopeless misery if they were called upon to do the work of the base. Those at the base would be utterly incompetent to carry on the duties of the higher strata. Our task is to ascertain what social conditions are the most harmonious to the desired end.

If we could ascertain by a study of heredity, or by an examination of all new-born babies, for what stratum they were the best adapted, we could then adjust their education to the position in life which they were best fitted to fulfil. But any such forecast is at present hopelessly beyond the power of science, and equally beyond the powers of discretion and judgment which would be needed in the inspectors who were to decide the lot of the infant. It is true, indeed, that just as men are unequal in adult life, so they are born unequal. In some the heredity is of the finest character; in others it is such as *cannot* lead to any real greatness. But the difficulty of discrimination is so overwhelming that for practical purposes we have to treat all new-born infants as being equal. In very extreme cases, such as congenital idiocy in the parents, it may very likely be proper to assume that the child will be fit only for the lowest type of work. But such cases must be rare, and do not affect the main contention. In any case we have no business to suppose that the children of the rich are con-

genitally better than the children of the poor.
Evidence may point in that direction in the
future, but at present there is none on which to
base an opinion. While recognising, then, that men
are born with very unequal potentialities, yet we
are obliged, by our inability to determine those
potentialities in advance, to rank them (with very
few exceptions) as all being equally fitted either
for the highest or for the lowest grades of labour.

So far we are in no particular opposition to
the average social reformer. The more ignorant
among them would perhaps hold that new-born
infants are actually equal in potentiality: the
Helvetian doctrine of a *tabula rasa* has still its
adherents among the class of reformers who have
never heard of Helvetius, and are unaware of the
discussions which have taken place on the subject.
But for practical purposes we have not yet differed
from the Socialist, for by admitting that all infants
must be regarded as equal we concede all that he
demands. The agreement does not last long,
however. The Socialist forthwith leaps to the
conclusion, summed up in the phrase " equality
of opportunity." By giving all children an equal
opportunity of advancing in the social scale we
provide (argues the Socialist) a natural test which
sorts out individuals and allows each one to fall
into that stratum which his true value indicates.

Once more we witness here the tendency to

think in terms of the individual—the cloven hoof of vicarious jealousy. It is *not* possible to determine during childhood in what individuals there will occur any particular efflorescence of genius. Spencer himself is an apt example. Under any system of equal opportunity he would, at any period of his childhood, have been marked out as unsuited for the higher strata of the social pyramid. For he was distinctly backward in his studies : he would have been massed with the majority, whose work in life lies at the base of the structure. It is scarcely more possible to determine during education the true bent of a child than it is to determine it immediately on birth. Genius is apt to be rebellious and individual; it is far removed from all relation to pedagogy; and the application to men of pedagogic standards necessarily issues in failure. The child of the highest pedagogic standard is not in any case the future genius. Moreover, this system involves an immense waste of social energy. If it is to have even a remote chance of success, equality of opportunity must be carried onward at least to university age ; and long before that time education begins to be specialised for the particular purpose to be filled in life. For those who are to work in the higher strata it has already been carried to a point far higher than is necessary or desirable in the case of those who have to work in the lower strata. For those who have to fill the great and responsible positions of society no expenditure of trouble or of money is too great to ensure their appropriate development. That expenditure is far greater than could possibly be devoted to *all* individuals. Moreover, since the great majority, by the conditions of our existence, have to do the lower types of work, it would be squandered on them. Worse still, it would render them unfit for and discontented with their humbler work. The effort to give to every child the training required to fulfil the highest kinds of work in later life is doomed to prove abortive, by reason of its very extravagance. Since only the few are needed for these higher kinds, it is doomed also to bring disappointment to the vast majority who are left over to carry on the humbler vocations. When for most of our social work what we want is carthorses, it is extravagant and brutal to train all individuals as racehorses and then to put them to the work of carthorses.

We are therefore thrown back upon *some* principle of selection. The requirement before us is that of training most men for the humbler work and a minority for the higher work. By what standard shall we decide upon the selection ? If researches into heredity make large practical advances in the future, we shall then perhaps have a satisfactory reply to this question. But so long

as we are obliged to regard all infants as alike in
their potentialities we have no guidance at all in
selection ; and it becomes a matter of complete
indifference what children are taken for the more
intensive lines of cultivation and what children
are left. It may then very well be abandoned to
the unfettered working of ordinary social laws.
Under those laws one comparatively small class
has all the opportunities ; the mass of the people
lack the higher training which is superfluous for
the work they have to do. The proportions
between these classes, when not interfered with
by legislation, seem to be well adapted to the
requirements, and in fact arise in consequence of
the requirements. Are they not then best left
alone ? The structure of society is not merely
haphazard and devoid of purpose : it exists
because it is adapted to the needs of society. We
have no guarantee that a different structure *would*
be adapted to the needs of society : we have no
reason to suppose that artificial social schemes
would work : we have, on the contrary, every
reason to suppose that, like the ideas of the average
inventor, unforeseen difficulties would lead to
ruin. The analogy is even stronger than it
appears ; for the difficulties cannot be regarded in
any way as unforeseen. They are only too patent.

It is certain that the main objections to this line
of argument come from sentiments rather than

reason, and from thinking in individuals rather than in societies. It will be pointed out that a class of idle rich is parasitic and offensive. True, it is a grave defect in the social system, but probably a necessary one. For it is necessary to have a wealthy class, whose existence is justified if it produces only a few who carry on the important work of society, which could not be done by the products of a poorer class. The riff-raff of the wealthier classes, constituting probably the majority, may well and rightly be objects of popular contempt ; but their numbers are insufficient to constitute any really perceptible burden on the backs of the workers. And as for the feeling of animosity against them by those who have to work, such feelings are inevitably a wrong motive of legislation. As already observed, the workers are in general aι least as happy as the idlers.

It must then be admitted that the conception of human equality is spurious, for the fundamental reason that the work of the world is extremely various and needs for its performance very varied types of men. In the conflict between *liberté* and *égalité*, *égalité* must within certain limits be abandoned. Yet this conclusion applies only to social and not to legislative equality. It is one of the most important principles of jurisprudence that all men are equal before the law ; it is a principle so well established that its defence would be an absurdity, and it has only to be stated. But when the law begins to ramify through every branch of social activity, carrying with it necessarily the principle of equality, then liberty begins to suffer. Equality is overdone, because legislation and government are too voluminous, too ubiquitous for a healthy community. Yet it is questionable whether such arguments as these lead to Spencer's conception of Administrative Nihilism. It may well be that the Governments of countries can do much valuable work, though on different lines to the efforts of the last half-century. Since it seems probable that after this war the need for economy will constitute an absolute bar to a further expansion of State functions in the direction of so-called social reform, we have to inquire whether the State shall contract again to its earlier impotence, or whether it shall branch out in new lines of progress.

The triumph of democracy would seem to indicate the latter view. And yet there is much to be said for the temporary quiescence of the European Governments. The exaggeration of the State idea leads, as Spencer was never tired of insisting, to a state of war. When men's ideas are constantly fixed upon the " State " or upon the " Government " as an agency which *does* things, wars are bound to be frequent. For chief among the things done by Governments is the

waging of wars; and the more men's eyes are
turned to their Governments—the more they enter
into the life and feelings of their Governments—the
more ready will they be to have their personal
sentiments raised by petty national differences,
which are not deserving the attention of the people
as a whole, and still less that utter absorption of
attention implied by war. On these grounds it
would appear a more wholesome social condition
when men are thinking more of their own affairs
in life and less of the affairs of the nation as a
whole, for by such means the welfare of the
nation is more likely to be achieved. The working
of the human body is not improved by fixing
attention on the workings of the various organs,
on respiration, on the beating of the heart, on the
action of the liver, etc. In the healthy state
the body works best when its various functions are
not the subject of too close attention and when a few
general rules of health only are carefully observed.
So the body politic seems to work best when its
separate parts are not subject to undue inspection
or interference by Government, but when legislation is limited to a few rigorous ordinances.

Spencer's final view of the functions and duties
of the State differed scarcely at all from his earlier
views. The first duty of the State is protection
against foreign aggression and the maintenance of
an army and navy adequate for that purpose;

the second duty is that of policing the country,
i.e., the protection of citizens against the aggression of other citizens, against crime, breach of
contract, etc. Beyond this the State should, in
Spencer's view, do nothing. " Every man is free
to do that which he wills, provided he infringes
not the equal freedom of any other man." The
construction and maintenance of roads, the Post
Office, education, factory laws, sanitary inspection
are all to be left to private enterprise. He never
suggested, of course, that the State should suddenly
abandon those branches of activity on which it
has long since embarked. Spencer did not believe
in sudden or revolutionary changes. Still less did
he hold that these services, which we have now
come to associate inseparably with the State,
should be left undone. On the contrary, the whole
tendency of his arguments was to show that they
would be far more efficiently and cheaply carried
out by corporations of private individuals. It is
always difficult to realise a state of affairs widely
different from that in which we live ; and with
many of these services it seems quite possible that
private enterprise would have been a far more
efficient mode of working them. Multitudinous
examples are piled up in all parts of Spencer's
works to show that private enterprise is more
efficient than public. In private concerns self-
interest is enlisted in favour of efficiency and

economy, and competition acts as a permanent
spur to improvement. Individuals are confronted
with the alternative of supplying well and cheaply
the public demand for some commodity, or else
of failure.   Public bodies are under no such
powerful incentive ; their services are run by
officials drawing fixed salaries, and driven by a
far less urgent stimulus than the private trader.
Moreover, they are frequently protected from
competition. Take, for instance, the Post Office.
Few people realise the heavy tax entailed by a
penny postage.   The cost of carrying a letter
from one part of London to another, for instance,
is a mere fraction of a penny. Were there no State
monopoly of letter carrying, Spencer conceives
two or more private post offices competing against
each other, cutting down their rates to the lowest
possible point, and raising to the highest efficiency
the rapidity of the conveyance.   There would be
a pillar-box in the wall of every house—a house-
to-house collection as well as a house-to-house
delivery. Nor can such a scheme be regarded as
altogether visionary ; for in fact where private
companies exist for the carriage of parcels they
are almost always cheaper than the parcel post,
notwithstanding the subsidy which they are
obliged to pay to the State for the privilege ; and
in London not only are the two or three competing
companies cheaper than the State service, but

they have long instituted a house-to-house collection, whereas you are required by the State service to carry your parcel to a post office yourself. And many people have observed that the civility and general amenities in the public post offices are inferior to those usual in private shops. There is not on the part of the Post Office officials the powerful stimulus of competition, which impels the private trader to meet the convenience of the public in every possible way. Post offices are almost the only kind of shops in the kingdom where you cannot run up a bill, but have to pay in cash over the counter for everything you purchase. But we are so accustomed to these impositions, that they are not realised as grievances. And so, Spencer argued, the same state of affairs exists wherever public bodies possess a monopoly in any branch of trade.

This is not the place to investigate the complex problems here raised. They are, after all, affairs of economics rather than of ethics. If Spencer's arguments are sound, not much more can be said than that they involve the public in a loss and inconvenience which, even if serious, can hardly have the moral importance which he endeavoured to ascribe to them. It may be true that the best railways in the world are in the hands of private companies, and that the worst are those owned as a State monopoly ; it may be true that Govern-

ment trading generally is costly and inefficient;
and yet there may be other arguments which out-
weigh those of pure economics. But in certain
other spheres Spencer's conclusions seem open to
a much more formidable criticism. He condemned
sanitary inspection by Government, for instance :
he considered that the maintenance of public
health was no part of the duties of Government.
This proposition will now be admitted by few.
Spencer imagined the existence of private companies of sanitary inspectors, who would carry
out any work brought to them at a far lower fee
than that now charged by way of taxation. He
imagined, further, a greater efficiency of sanitary
inspection by private companies. For a company
which once made a mistake—passed an insanitary
dwelling as healthy—would immediately be ruined ;
the public would in future straightway resort to
rival companies. A mistake by a private inspect-
ing company would be far more impossible than
by a Government company, where nothing more
serious would ensue than hostile criticism. And
Spencer fortified his arguments, with his usual
brilliance, by citing innumerable instances of the
follies of public inspectors and of the ill-success
which had attended all efforts to suppress disease.
In many of these criticisms he was well justified.
In one of them—namely, the Contagious Diseases
Act—educated opinion has almost unanimously

come round to his belief that the attempt to combat these diseases by Government inspection cannot succeed.

Yet the arguments on the other side seem even more conclusive. If there were no compulsory sanitary inspection, then it would be open to the poorer or stupider people to live in insanitary places. Spencer would allow a man's ignorance or obstinacy to stand in the way of his protection from disease ; so long, indeed, as his insanitary conditions did not endanger his neighbours.

It is very easy, and in these days very popular, to criticise Spencer's demand for the self-effacement of the State. Yet we must not forget that in the state of knowledge attained when he wrote the advice was probably better founded than most people would care to admit. But knowledge continues to advance in a series of geometrical progression. Science has at length placed in our hands weapons for dealing with our environment, of a potency undreamt of half a century ago. These mighty weapons cannot be wielded by private citizens ; they require all the strength, wealth, and power of the State. If the State does not wield them, they must remain unused. There are more cogent arguments for State activity now than there ever were in Spencer's time. The war against disease for instance, is not the war of a class, or of a section, or of a majority of the people.

It is a war of the whole people, and in the immediate interests of every citizen in the land. Nor is it war *against* any foreign nation, or section, or class of the people ; it is a war against the common enemy of all mankind and of every individual born into the world. And in its mental aspects it is equally to be desired. For it is not based upon passion, hate, or jealousy ; it does not cultivate emotions of violence and disorder. It constitutes in itself an object lesson in the power and beneficence of science ; it leads to a mental elevation towards general philanthropy rather than to the anti-social results of war of the mediæval kind.

It is hard to condemn Spencer's views in our present state of knowledge, for they have never been put to the test. The period in history when they were most nearly realised was perhaps the most flourishing period of progress that there has ever been. Yet we must remember that he wrote for his times, and when public ideals were very different from what they are now. For the 'forties and 'fifties of last century his theories probably did represent the best line of social progress. But Spencer's mind became dogmatic as he grew older—and his theories froze into a solid framework which resisted all modification by newer ideas and by greater knowledge. We cannot admit that the dogmas of the 'fifties are the last word in the science of sociology or in the art of ethics. Yet one thing we may with advantage carry forward, not only into this century, but as a permanent part of our acquired civilisation. That thing is the ideal of liberty, which must constitute the background from which all our social theories and all our legislation must start. We cannot define it in a formula, as Spencer attempted to do ; we cannot establish hard and fast restrictions upon the activities of the State. Liberty should not be a dogma, but should constitute the atmosphere of social and political thought. We may not like many of the applications of the doctrine of liberty which were emphasised by Spencer and Mill; but that does not invalidate the doctrine itself. Just as Spencer's own doctrines became hardened by dogmas and formulæ, so there is a danger that progress in the body politic may be arrested by laws and formulæ which freeze society into its existing form. The fluidity maintained by freedom allows the natural changes of social order to advance unimpeded. It does not tie men to those particular ideals which are peculiar to any special age. Only a country which is steadily animated by the great ideal of freedom can hope to escape that degeneration of old age which in the body politic, as in the body physical, comes on by the slow dissemination of rigidity and unadaptability throughout the tissues of the organism.

CHAPTER VI

THIS is by far the longest single work written by Spencer. It occupies three stout volumes, of which the first alone contains nearly 900 pages.

"THE DATA OF SOCIOLOGY."

Part i. deals with "The Data of Sociology," and occupies in itself 432 pages. The earlier volumes of the Philosophy are devoted to Organic Evolution. Spencer now deals with what he calls Super-Organic Evolution, that is to say, Evolution, not of single individuals, but of societies consisting of many individuals. The factors concerned in this super-organic evolution are divisible (according to Spencer) into two main groups— the external and the internal. The external factors are such as climate, the surface of the earth, the fauna and flora. The internal factors are those arising from the physical, intellectual, and emotional characteristics of the men and women who constitute the society in question.

Dealing first with the external factors it is obvious that social evolution is impossible outside

certain limitations of heat and cold. The earliest
forms of society arose in hot climates, and in
countries where the means of existence were
abundant ; so that much spare energy was available for social progress. In some countries, such
as India, carnivores and reptiles stood in the
way of evolution. In others, pastoral life may be
prevented by insects, such as the tsetse fly in
Africa, or agricultural life by swarms of insects
which devour the crops.

Turning to the internal factors, we come first
to the physical characteristics of primitive man.
There is, Spencer says, reason to believe that he
was smaller in stature than civilised man, and had a
lower muscular development and physical strength.
His alimentary system, on the other hand, was
larger ; for his food was inferior in quality, and
the supply irregular, demanding a greater capacity
for digesting large amounts when it was available.
On the other hand, he was hardier than civilised
man and much more tolerant of pain. He arrived
earlier at maturity.

Passing to the emotional characteristics of
primitive man, impulsiveness is a striking feature.
Emotion tends to pass straightway into action ;
and the character is inconstant, fickle, and im-
provident. Sociality is poorly developed, and
regulation of conduct weak. All the sympathetic
sentiments reach a low development only ; and

the higher forms, such as that of justice, are very rudimentary. Fixity of habit is very strong : there is dislike of novelty ; and the emotional life flows to the concrete, with little development of any of the higher or more abstract sentiments.

Intellectually, primitive man resembles the children of civilised man. Primitive men are absorbed in sensation and preception to the detriment of higher intellectual qualities. Their senses are more acute than those of the civilised. They are unable to concentrate their attention for long on any one thing, but are quickly exhausted. They have great imitative powers, but low capacity for generalisation, or for passing beyond the region of isolated facts. They show little aptitude for being surprised, and small curiosity ; but on the other hand are exceedingly credulous, believing any story, however monstrous, and adopting any explanation, however absurd.

We arrive now at the main thesis of " The Data of Sociology " namely, a theory as to the origin of the idea of spirits, and of religions in general. The occurrence of unaccountable events gives rise to the notion of a general arbitrariness of Nature ; sudden appearances and disappearances suggesting a duality of existence. This suggestion is fortified by dreams. During sleep primitive man passes through experiences which he imagines to be real. He seems to visit various places, and talk to various people, while all the time his friends tell him his body has been lying still. He thus jumps to the conclusion of a dual personality : he thinks he has a soul which has wandered away from his body and returns when he awakes. The belief that he has a double is strengthened by observation of his shadow—an intangible, inexplicable being which seems to accompany him about. His reflection in still water further bears out the idea of duality ; and the Basuto will not walk by a stream, lest a crocodile should seize his shadow or reflection. In swoon, apoplexy, etc., the double may depart for longer periods before returning to the body ; and in death the possibility of its future return is still entertained.

The double is at first conceived as a facsimile of the original. It is liable to hunger, thirst, etc. ; it may have an accident, or it may itself be killed. On the death of a man food, drink, weapons, etc., are buried with him for the use of his double ; and his wives may be sacrificed for the same purpose. After a time the number of ghosts thus originating begins to accumulate, until at length every unaccountable event is set down to their instrumentality. Disease is regarded as the work of a spirit which has taken up its abode in the patient's body ; and attempts are made to exorcise it by horrible grimaces, or abominable stenches, or by thrashing the patient so that his body should become an uncomfortable habitat. On the other hand, they may be dealt with by propitiatory measures—by prayers, offerings, etc. ; from which arises the practice of worship.

We arrive now at Spencer's final elaboration of the " ghost theory," or the theory that all forms of religious observances have grown from the worship of the souls of deceased ancestors. In some cases it is supposed that the souls of the departed may inhabit manufactured effigies ; hence the worship of idols. Or they may enter into other inanimate objects, giving origin to fetishism. Animal worship arises in a similar way. Snakes, owls, etc., haunting a house which was inhabited by the deceased may by a very natural superstition be supposed to harbour the spirit of the deceased, and may subsequently come to be worshipped for their own sake, when the origin of the practice has been forgotten. The common habit of giving animal nicknames to chiefs would also generate animal worship. A powerful chief is supposed to retain his power, or even to gain an increased power, after his death. He is therefore an object for general propitiation. If the chief had been known by some such nickname as the " Lion " or the " Bull," the propitiation offered in that name would be supposed by later generations to be directed to the animals themselves ; for primitive speech easily lends itself to confusion of this kind.

Hence in Spencer's opinion there would ultimately arise a genuine animal worship.

Plant worship and Nature worship have a similar origin. Worship of the " Dawn " would develop, as above described, from propitiation of the ghost of a deceased ancestor, who had been so nick-named, possibly because he was born early in the morning. Worship of the sun is of the same character, the nickname in this case being due either to the exalted position of the deceased warrior, or to a birth name, or to the fact that he belonged to a conquering family which had first turned up from the East.

From the idea of ghosts, thus conceived, Spencer deduces all ideas of deities, not excluding that of the Hebrew religion. The deities, at first held to be exact duplicates of living men, gradually become more refined and rarefied, till they develop into the gods of civilised nations. Fasting arises from the practice of setting apart one's food for the use of the soul of the departed. Sacrifices, offerings, etc., are similarly accountable. Temples, altars, and so on grow from the mounds of earth thrown over the body of the dead man ; these mounds being intended either to protect his soul from wandering carnivores and the accidents of Nature or to keep his soul securely buried underground and prevent it from sallying forth to disturb the lives of younger generations.

The above is a brief description of the " Ghost
theory " of the origin of religious beliefs. Criticism
upon it may take the form of a suggestion that,
while Spencer unquestionably set forward *one*
and perhaps the most important factor in the
origin of religions, there are probably many
other contributory factors which he failed to
recognise. It is characteristic of his mind to
compel *all* the facts to conform to the one principle which filled his attention at the time. Just
as he was prepared to base organic evolution on
one factor only, and that one now held even by
the few who support it to be at most a minor
factor, so he was to such an extent obsessed by
his ghost theory that he was quite incapable of
admitting the existence of any other element.

But a still more cogent line of criticism might be
advanced. Spencer endeavoured to think himself into the mind of the savage, and thereupon
to argue out the inferences which a savage would
draw from the various phenomena which came
under his observation. And he defends the ghost
theory on the ground that, in the particular intellectual state which primitive man had reached, the
hypothesis of survival and gods was the most
rational open to him. These superstitions in fact
offered the most logical theory, to the primitive
mind, in explanation of the surrounding universe.

Now it may be argued that the problem is not

one of logic at all, but of psychology. Men in general, and especially primitive men, do not reach their conclusions by any process of intellect or logic, but by emotional bent. Spencer may correctly have indicated the process of reasoning most natural to a primitive man, *if they did reason.* In his efforts to read himself into their minds he has only partially succeeded: he has to some extent assumed *their* methods of thought, but to a greater extent endowed them with his own. He depicts them rather as miniature Spencers, and their mythology as a miniature Synthetic Philosophy. He has found it impossible, or perhaps omitted to attempt, to realise the emotional condition of primitive man. Yet it is one of the most fundamental truths of psychology that any emotion tends to call up in imagination objects which are agreeable to that emotion. A person suffering from melancholia sees in all the events of life threats to his safety and happiness. A person under the influence of powerful fear sees in his environment nothing but terrifying objects. If a man is in love with a commonplace woman, and someone remarks that she possesses some peculiar virtue, he is very likely to believe it without further criticism. If he has the undisciplined mind of a savage, he is quite certain to believe it. We now as a nation have a powerful emotion of dislike to the Germans. If anyone were to suggest some evil attribute of the German mind, most of us would receive the suggestion with acclamation; but if anyone were to suggest a noble attribute, we should demand full proof, and even then should not be very ready to accept or repeat it. And if we were primitive men the tendency would be far more overwhelming than it is. In short, for any undisciplined mind only two conditions are needed for establishing a belief: (1) A pre-existent emotion, which the belief would gratify; (2) a suggestion. If the suggestion is in harmony with the emotion or gratifies the emotion, belief ensues. The suggestion may be of the most casual and trifling description:

> "Trifles light as air
> Are to the jealous confirmations strong
> As proofs of holy writ."

Now the state of mind of the savage is predominantly emotional, to an extent which we can hardly conceive. He knows none of that intellectual and critical discipline which is possessed in some degree by the most ignorant of civilised men. His emotional condition is one that encourages every sort of strong conviction; his intellectual faculties of criticism are almost absent. The slightest suggestion that harmonises with his raw and aboriginal emotions is received with the most bigoted credulity. The ground is almost infinitely fertile; and there is no intellectual husbandman to rake out the weeds which fall upon it. The most conflicting and absurd beliefs are simultaneously entertained, so long as they satisfy the single condition of being agreeable to the emotions natural to his constitution.

Under these circumstances it is irrelevant to inquire, as Spencer did, into the source of the suggestion which leads the savage to his myth. The one relevant factor is the emotional state of mind which makes him ready and eager to embrace that myth. How it started, how the original suggestion occurred, is nothing: the most casual remark, the most fleeting thought, the whistle of the wind in the branches of a tree, would suffice. Anything or nothing: we can never know, nor can it ever matter to us. How is it that some card-players think that luck attends certain seats or a certain colour of the cards? It is merely a suggestion which, falling on fruitful ground, instantly generates a tendency to believe. This particular suggestion has in fact produced a sort of half-belief in a certain proportion of card-players. But to *explain* the superstition we should surely never enter into a detailed inquiry as to how the suggestion was first made; and if we ever could make the discovery, it would help us not a whit in comprehending the superstition. For the superstition is attributable wholly to *emotional* factors not to any process of logic or intellect.

And so it is with primitive man. In seeking
the *logical* antecedents of their myths, Spencer
was after a Will-o'-the-wisp. The suggestion which
originally introduced the germ of those myths
must inevitably be lost in obscurity, and in any
case is irrelevant ; for if that particular suggestion
had not occurred, some other closely resembling
it would have served as the starting-point. Many
such must occur even in one ordinary day of
a savage's life. The relevant and fundamental
factor is a sort of primitive " will to believe "—
an emotional ground on which certain kinds of
seeds flourish luxuriously. If we are studying the
reproduction of plants, we do not think it necessary to trace the particular pollen-grain which
sets up fertilisation in a given case. It behoves
us only to know from what species or variety of
plant it came. The air is full of such pollen-grains :
the wind blows them about in unaccountable ways,
and finally one of them lands on a stigma ripe to
receive it, and the rest follows. The precise
journey of the pollen-grain, its isolation from all
other pollen-grains of the same variety, is beside
our point, in addition to being a difficult and
unprofitable investigation.

Spencer then appears to have committed what
may be called a heuristic error of method. The
gods of primitive men are the creations of their
emotions ; and in all cases their gods have the

qualities which excite and enhance those emotions.
A savage is subject to no emotion so constant
as that of fear. Accordingly he entertains a belief
in gods, ghosts, and every sort of supernatural
being, which have this in common—that they
instil fear. Feelings of obedience and reverence
are common to many primitive peoples, and are
intensified by the political conditions under which
they live. And these emotions quickly raise up,
from any slight and fortuitous suggestion, supernatural beings which demand and enhance the
tendencies to obedience and reverence. Just as
the roaring lion walks about " seeking whom he
may devour," so the submissive spirit goes about
seeking whom he may obey. The readiness of
the emotions, the total absence of a critical faculty
—these are the prerequisites. Then the first
chance suggestion acts like a spark, to start off the
train which develops into the ultimate myth.
Everywhere the type of myth is a certain index of
the state of mind. Jealousy gives rise to a " jealous
god." The tender emotions produce a god of love.
Moral emotions establish a god who enjoins moral
codes, and enforces them by punishments, which
are savage or mild, according as the emotions of
primitive man are cruel or gentle. The emotions are
first : they are part of the physical constitution
of man ; and given the emotions, given the absence
of a critical faculty, the mythology is inevitable.

Spencer's discussion of " The Data of Sociology " concludes with a chapter on the scope
of the Science of Sociology. The first division
of the science, according to his treatment, is the
study of Domestic Institutions, with an account
of the result upon social evolution, of the various
forms of domestic life. Next come the three
forms of Regulative Institutions, political, ecclesiastical, and ceremonial, the last of these dealing
with the minor forms of control exercised by
public opinion. Finally Industrial and Professional
Organisation have to be dealt with. But before
coming to these main divisions of the work we
have still (in accordance with the general plan of
the Philosophy) to give an account of " The Inductions of Sociology," to which Part ii. of " The
Principles of Sociology " is devoted.

" The Inductions of Sociology."

These Inductions take the form of a detailed
comparison between the body politic and the body
physical. They constitute a description of the
social organism, with its points of resemblance to
and difference from the individual organism.

The analogy between the two arises from the
single circumstance that in each the different
parts are mutually dependent. In the social
organism this dependence is expressed by division
of labour. In the physical organism there is

likewise the " physiological division of labour " : each organ is developed for the performance of some special function necessary to the general life of the organism. The individual, moreover, consists of a vast aggregation of living cells, just as the social organism consists of a population of separate individuals. The most cardinal difference between the two arises from the fact that whereas, in the individual, consciousness is concentrated in a small part of the nervous system, in the social organism it is equally diffused throughout the whole of the individuals constituting the society.

Growth is manifested by both kinds of organism ; and in both it may be effected either by the union of previously separate organisms, or by interstitial growth—by multiplication of the cells in the one case, and of the individuals in the other, so as to increase the size of the body, physical or politic.

In animals of low types, there is very little struc- ture ; organs are lacking, and there is comparative homogeneity throughout. So it is in societies of low type; they are little more than mere collections of individuals. But as these societies advance they acquire great heterogeneity and com- plexity corresponding to the heterogeneity and complexity of evolved animals. In early stages each individual is comparatively self-sufficient ; in later stages he becomes differentiated, in so far that he devotes himself and becomes specially adapted to one particular kind of work, while trusting to the remainder of the community to supply his other needs. Moreover, those engaged in the same kind of work congregate in particular places—as, for instance, spinners at Oldham, or cutlers at Sheffield. So, too, in an animal, cells performing the same function are aggregated together to form an organ, as, for instance, the liver. The social organism, like the individual, can produce offspring in the form of colonies, which straightway assume the developed structural characteristics of their parentage.

The first main differentiation to appear in an evolving society is that between the regulative and the operative activities. One class, that of the warriors, becomes adapted to purposes of offence and defence, as well as of government ; the other becomes industrial and is devoted to the sustentation of the society. In this we see a correspondence with animal development. On the one hand there are the structures for ensuring the safety and preservation of the animal ; on the other hand there is the alimentary system for sustaining it. Between these two there evolves later a distributing system in each.

In the social organism the distributing system is represented by railways, roads, tracks, etc., along which commodities travel from that part of the organism where they are produced to that where they are needed. In animals this function is carried out by the vascular system, which carries the digested nutriment to all parts of the body. Even the pulsations in the blood-flow are paralleled by the alternate increases and decreases of traffic from hour to hour, day to day, week to week, etc. Just as the main arterial and venous vessels are endowed with walls which sharply limit and define the course of the blood, so the main railways and roads are sharply marked off by lines or fences from the surrounding country. As the blood-vessels become smaller, their routes become less definite and less rigidly enclosed, until we reach the capillary vessels which have no defined path. So in the social distributing agencies, the smaller roads are often not fenced and less sharply marked off from the adjacent land, until we reach the country paths and tracks which have neither permanency nor definiteness.

The regulative system consists, in the social organism, of the governmental-military agencies ; and in the individual organism of the nervo-muscular apparatus. The nervous system, like the governmental agency, consists of a hierarchy of nervous centres subordinate to one another. The simpler kind of stimuli are met by an immediate response of a lower centre, as in reflex action. The more complex pass up to higher centres, whose decisions are conveyed by means of nerve fibres

to the muscles which have to be actuated. These
nerve fibres themselves are analogous to telegraph
wires in the social organism. In primitive animals
an impulse passes slowly from one part to another
—as news passes slowly in a primitive society.
With evolution the passage of the impulses
becomes defined by fixed routes and along fixed
structures.   In animals the volume of blood
passing along a vessel is controlled by the vaso-
motor nerves which run along the vessel-walls,
and which can produce contraction or expansion
of the lumen of the vessel. So, too, in the social
organism, the railways are accompanied by telegraph wires, which serve to control and regulate
the amount of traffic which passes. Both nerve and
telegraph wire have to be insulated ; and where
the telegraph is laid underground, the wires are
collected into bundles, each single wire having its
insulating sheath—just as nerves in their myelin
sheaths also run in bundles within other sheaths.

After describing thus the analogy between the
individual and social organism, we are introduced
to two modes in which societies may be classified.
According to the first mode, they are arranged
according to their degree of composition as simple,
compound, doubly-compound, and trebly-com-
pound. The simple societies are those which are
completely homogeneous, and not formed by the
fusion of other societies. The various forms of

compound societies are those formed by the fusion, mainly as a result of conquest, of two or more different societies.

The second mode of classification is into the two groups of military and industrial. The militant types of society are those in which the structures of offence and defence are highly developed, and in which social life is carried on by *compulsory* co-operation. The industrial types are those in which the military predominance is reduced, and in which social life is carried on by *voluntary* co-operation. The militant type is encouraged and developed by international conflicts and preparations for war; the industrial type is a product of peace. Metamorphoses occur in societies from time to time; they oscillate from the one type to the other, according as the times are of peace or war.

With this doctrine "The Inductions of Sociology" come to an end; and we pass to the remaining divisions of "The Principles of Sociology," in which we are shown what deductions may be drawn, in the light of the foregoing principles, and of the law of evolution.

"DOMESTIC INSTITUTIONS."

The first subject to be dealt with is "Domestic Institutions." Spencer had already shown in

"The Principles of Biology" that an antagonism
exists between individuation and reproduction,
between the interests of parents and the interests
of the species. It follows that the highest constitution of the family is that in which the duties
of parenthood detract least from the individual
lives of the parents. This end is achieved in three
ways—by a longer period of life antecedent to
marriage ; by the production of fewer offspring,
which, however, in view of diminished infantile
mortality, is adequate to the requirements of the
species ; and by the lengthening of life, after the
reproductive age has passed.

The primitive relations of the sexes were
characterised by indefiniteness and incoherence.
There are, says Spencer, at first no settled forms of
relationship whatever ; and various primitive races
furnish illustrations of every kind of sexual relation
—promiscuity, polyandry, polygyny, and monogamy. The practice of exogamy—the custom,
that is, of taking a wife from some other tribe than
that to which the man belongs—arises among warlike peoples, where the capture of women belonging
to the enemy constitutes a trophy of victory and
valour. From this origin there is established a
strong sentiment in favour of exogamous unions,
and a contempt, rising to moral reprobation, of
marriage within the clan. The custom ultimately
extends to cover union with any woman of a

different tribe, even though not captured in battle.

Endogamy, on the other hand, arises, according to Spencer, among weaker tribes. If any member of such a tribe were to seize women of another tribe, retribution would follow. The tribe from whom the women had been taken would attack the tribe of their capturer and bring upon it the calamities of war. Hence the establishment of a powerful sentiment in favour of endogamy.

Promiscuity and polyandry are both characteristic of primitive peoples. They naturally lead to a low idea of the family, and are opposed to the welfare of the children. Doubt as to the paternity of the children involves the reckoning of inheritance through the female line. Polyandry, nevertheless, is of service where a paucity of food stands in the way of rapid multiplication. Polygyny, or the marriage of one man with several women, is a higher institution ; for both parents of the children are known, and, descent being through the male line, a form of ancestor-worship becomes possible. In a tribe of warlike habits polygyny is useful as conducing to a more rapid multiplication, which makes good the incessant losses among the warriors of the tribe. Far higher than any of these forms of union, however, stands monogamy, which arises when the sexes become more equalised owing to diminution of war. Whether or not

monogamy is the natural form of human marriage,
it has for a long time past been growing innate in
civilised peoples.

Polygyny is the natural form of marriage in
militant societies—partly, as already said, owing
to the paucity of warriors and the large demand
for replenishing the population ; partly owing to
the habit of seizing the women of the enemy.
Monogamy, on the other hand, is proper to an
industrial State—where, indeed, polygyny is
impracticable, for there is no adequate surplus
in the number of women.

Passing to the social aspects of the family,
Spencer finds that at first there was no settled
headship, any more than there were settled
marital relations.   After a time, however, the
patriarchal system appears—groups of pastoral
people allied together by kinship, and following
the family chief or patriarch.   By coalescence
of several such patriarchal groups compound
societies are formed : all the largest and most
advanced societies have originated in this way.
As the various family groups become more closely
integrated into societies, there takes place an
accompanying disintegration within each family.
The unit of the State, which at first was the
family, becomes at length the individual.   It
seems, Spencer adds, that this break-up of the family
has in some cases already gone too far.   There is,

however, a sharp distinction between family-ethics and State-ethics. In families it is necessary that each individual should receive attention in proportion to his incapacity; for this is obviously essential with children at different ages. In the State, however, the law must be that each individual receives a reward that is proportionate to his merit and ability. Much mischievous legislation arises from a confusion of the two.

An inquiry into the *status* of women and of children elicits the truth that their *status* is low in proportion as the society is militant, and high in proportion as it is industrial. Polygyny, which, as already seen, is associated with militancy, involves a low *status* of women, because they are compelled to do the servile work. Moreover, the despotic modes of government prevalent in militant societies are associated with despotic modes of government within the family itself. The *status* both of women and children regularly improves as the compulsory co-operation of militant societies gives way to the voluntary co-operation of industrial societies. "Domestic Institutions" ends with a chapter on "Domestic Retrospect and Prospect" in the course of which it is foreshadowed that as societies pass more and more from a military to an industrial state the system of monogamy will be further extended and strengthened, though it will be made to rest upon the tie of affection rather than a tie of law.   The *status* of women will at the same time continue to be raised.   Their social disabilities will be removed, although for the present it is undesirable that they should attain a political equality with men : partly because they do not bear the military responsibilities which belong to men, and partly because they are more devoted to authority, and less affected by the higher sentiments of justice and freedom ; so that entire political equality is undesirable until the complete stage of industrialism has been attained.

" CEREMONIAL INSTITUTIONS."

We now reach the second volume of " The Principles of Sociology," which opens with an investigation into " Ceremonial Institutions." These constitute the earliest form of control of human conduct—from which are derived those more definite forms of control exercised by State and Church.   Moreover, although they appear now to be entirely arbitrary, they all, in Spencer's opinion, take their origin from some act of real utility. Advancing towards the enemy carrying the green boughs of a tree has, for instance, come to be recognised as a sign of pacific intentions ; but the custom first arose from the desire to show that no weapons were being carried—a fact which the enemy would be unable to see, unless something else were carried which precluded the holding of a weapon. In general, ceremonial observances emanate from the relations of the conquered to the conqueror. Trophies possessed by a warrior symbolise his prowess in fighting the enemy; and from trophy-taking arise the various customs of mutilation. The victor, instead of slaying his opponent and then cutting off some part of his body as a trophy, spares his life but still mutilates him to preserve a record of his victory. At length mutilation comes to be a symbol of subservience; and it is practised in order to propitiate not only living chiefs, but also the dead chiefs who have become deified. Circumcision arose in this way, and not for the reasons commonly alleged. Furthermore, the sacrifice either to a god or man of some part of the body is supposed to endow the recipient with peculiar supernatural powers over the individual mutilated.

The custom of giving presents likewise originates, according to Spencer, in a desire to propitiate. When these presents are laid by the tomb of the dead we have the rudiments of religious sacrifice. The presents of meat, drink, clothes, etc., at length becomes a purely ceremonial and arbitrary practice, from which springs the whole system of the Church revenues. And just as presents to gods are the origin of ecclesiastical revenues, so presents to living rulers are the origin of political revenues. The custom of visiting originates from that of giving presents ; for such presents involve the necessity of carrying them to the recipient. Obeisances were originally modes of expressing submission to a conqueror by prostration before him ; and also of professing pleasure at his presence. All forms of obeisance and greetings are derived by abbreviation of the original prostration, as, for instance, in kneeling down while at prayer. Submission involved, moreover, the handing over of all one's possessions, including even clothes, to the conqueror. Nakedness is an original symbol of subordination ; and by gradual curtailment and refinement we arrive at the custom in civilised society of taking off one's hat to indicate respect. The ruler is further propitiated by kissing, at first his feet, then his hands. The modern shake of the hands is derived from a simultaneous attempt of each individual to raise the other's hand to his mouth in order to kiss it, counteracted by the attempt of the other to refuse this sign of humility. The various forms of address are similarly derived from propitiatory formulæ, some of which indeed still preserve traces of their origin, as in the termination of a letter by " Your obedient servant."

Spencer carried his passion for logical origins to an explanation of titles. An individual was known by some peculiarity in his appearance, and the title thence bestowed upon him developed into a proper name. The title " god," for instance, was at first associated with the meaning " father." Titles, moreover, tend to become degraded by constant application to a larger group of individuals. In French, for instance, " *sire* " was at first a title limited to rulers. As it gradually became extended to larger classes of persons, *seigneur*, abbreviated into *sieur*, took its place as a form of respect. This again was extended to more and more people, till *monsieur* was introduced to fulfil its original meaning. This also has now become universalised, as has the English " esquire."

Badges, again, are said by Spencer to be descended from trophies. The military flag or ensign is derived from a spear which very commonly carried upon it some decoration. It was found convenient for the spear of the commander to bear some particularly conspicuous decoration, so that his men might know where he was ; and hence is derived the coloration of flags. The wearing of clothes, moreover, was originally adopted to gain admiration—more particularly as nudity was a symbol of subjection. The various signs of class distinction similarly spring from origins of a significant and not an arbitrary character. Fashion is based upon imitation. The imitation is in part propitiatory, as where subjects imitate their ruler, and partly competitive ; each class endeavouring to elevate itself by imitating the procedure of those of higher rank.

Regarding ceremonial institutions as a whole, Spencer finds that their development is most conspicuous in militant societies and least conspicuous in industrial societies. In militant societies the restraints imposed by ceremony are powerful and widespread. The *régime* of compuslory co-operation naturally lends itself to this fundamental class of restrictions on freedom. Fashion alone, in so far as it is based upon a demand for equality, is an offshoot of the industrial system. Militant societies are eminently characterised by profound obeisances, elaborate forms of address, etc., etc.; in mixed societies these usages still obtain most among the ruling and military classes. As the industrial type of society continues to supersede the militant type, we may anticipate a progressive disuse of all these ceremonial forms. The change, however, should take place gradually; for only as human nature becomes more perfect can it dispense with the class of restrictions here dealt with.

" POLITICAL INSTITUTIONS."

From " Ceremonial " Spencer now passes on to " Political Institutions." At the outset a warning is given against importing prejudice into our investigations. We must be prepared to find that certain kinds of political institutions which we hold in deep abhorrence have nevertheless contributed in the past to the formation and integration of complex societies.

The benefits of social life arise from the fact of co-operation, different duties being undertaken by the different elements of the society. This co-operation is of two main kinds—voluntary and compulsory. Voluntary co-operation is that which results without any conscious intention, but entirely from the pursuit by individuals of their own private interests. Compulsory co-operation is a form of organisation established by agencies of Government : it is with this form of co-operation that political institutions are concerned. The existence of any established form of organisation is valuable as maintaining order in the community, but constitutes an obstacle in the way of progress or change, and hinders growth.

The growth or integration of societies is determined by various conditions. It begins when one tribe robs another of its women, or captures and enslaves its men. It proceeds by enslavement and annexation on a larger scale. It is, however, limited by various circumstances, such as the physical character of the country and its capacity for holding large social groups. Moreover, the amount of cohesion in a society is dependent upon the homogeneity of its component parts.

A society composed of groups of divergent characteristics will hold loosely together and easily become disintegrated ; whereas a firmer cohesion will be attained where the individuals are comparatively alike. The main cause of political and social integration, however, is war. Where several tribes unite for the purpose of carrying on a war, they become habituated to constant organisation and control, and therefore more fitted to constitute a coherent group. The enforced union, established by military organisation, involves a loss of individual freedom ; which is not restored until that later period of development, when the voluntary co-operation of the industrial State is adequate to take the place of the compulsory co-operation of the militant State.

Dealing with political differentiation, class-divisions are found to exist at the beginnings of social life. They first exhibit the form of a subordination of women. Then a slave class is formed by captures from neighbouring tribes. When the agricultural stage is reached, it becomes possible to conquer an entire people as well as the land which they inhabit : the conquered people then become serfs ; and it is not the case that serfdom is a mitigated form of slavery. The militant class, being by force of arms the dominant class, acquire possession of the land ; and the connection between militancy and landownership survives through long stages of social evolution. The various class differences thus initiated become confirmed and strengthened by habit; each grade becomes habituated to its own surroundings. The chief factor in the break-up of these class distinctions is the rise of industrialism, under which wealth accruing to various members of the proletariat establishes a competition with the power of the militant classes. Moreover, as the wealth of industry is not based upon subordination of classes, but upon free contract, the factor leading to subordination gradually weakens. As Sir Henry Maine put it, the *régime* of *contract* follows and takes the place of the *régime* of *status*.

From the earliest times political organisation shows signs of a triple division. In a primitive tribe, when some public question, perhaps of defence or of migration, has to be decided, a conference would take place of all the individuals of the tribe. The great majority of these, however, would be listeners rather than speakers. The actual discussion would be carried on by a certain number of the older or more distinguished warriors, who would thus come to form a sort of oligarchy possessing more influence and power than the rest. Among these, again, there would most likely be one who had greater influence than any other, and would in course of time come to be regarded as the chief of the tribe. We find, therefore, the germs of a general assembly, a council, and a king ; and, according to the conditions in which the society is placed, one or other of these elements becomes the preponderant power. Nevertheless the force, which resides behind the political forms whatever they may be, is always the same— namely, popular sentiment. The power of a king, however absolute, consists in the correlative orientation of the minds of his subjects. Despotism, as much as democracy, is a product of the mental attitude of the people who live under it.

Passing now to the separate elements of this universal triune organisation, the evidence shows that the primitive political head is either a pre-eminent warrior or pre-eminent medicine-man. At first the headship is unsettled ; but as the hereditary principle becomes recognised the kingship becomes more stable. The idea that departed chiefs have become gods, who continue to exercise power over the fortunes of men, naturally causes special reverence to be devoted to their sons. The autocracy thus established, notwithstanding its evils, is a factor very favourable for the integration or closer union of the governed people. Compound political heads or directive councils are likewise formed when several tribes unite for purposes of military co-operation. The essential fact in all kinds of society, however, is that the structure of the society was not consciously or purposely established, but that it evolved or grew by natural processes to its ultimate state, without any conscious endeavour of its own.

Consultative and representative bodies are next considered ; and the conclusion is reached that the former have evolved from the primitive council of war, while the latter begin to flourish when wars cease to be chronic and the industrial *régime* develops. The evolution of military systems is shown to be towards a gradual decrease of the proportion of the society devoted to military pursuits, starting from the time when the whole society constituted an army and the non-combatant sections were exclusively occupied in the sustenance of the warriors. At the same time, the army, reduced greatly in size, becomes a standing army, instead of being disbanded at the conclusion of war. Moreover, military organisation within the army gradually increases. In the primitive kind of battles fighting consisted merely of a vast number of duels between individual soldiers of the contending tribes ; and the leaders themselves were mainly occupied during a battle in individual combats.

Judicial and executive systems have arisen from the primitive gatherings of people, head-men, and chief ; laws originate from the supposed commands of deceased ancestors, and were thus

formerly of the nature of religious precepts.
Property has passed from a state of communal
ownership to a state of individual ownership as the
industrial system has gradually supplanted the
military system.   Revenue has a two-fold origin.
Direct taxation, as shown in " Ceremonial Institutions," is derived from propitiatory and voluntary offerings, which ultimately became permanent
and compulsory.   Indirect taxation arose from
the habit of taking from traders a portion of their
goods in return for permission to trade.   These
contributions were also at first voluntary offerings
of the traders ; but subsequently the Government
adopted the practice of seizing them as a right.

The main conclusion, however, that emerges
from " Political Institutions " is that societies
exhibit one or other of two main and fundamentally
opposed types—the militant type and the industrial type.   The militant type, characterised by
universal compulsory co-operation, in the highest
degree subordinates the individual to the State.
The entire community is divided into the army and
the non-combatants who sustain the army ; and
the tendency is to increase the army and reduce
the non-combatant section to the farthest practicable limit.   The form of government in militant
societies is typically despotic.   The nation, both
combatant and non-combatant, is governed by
a hierarchy of officers ; and obedience is held to

be one of the highest virtues. Patriotism reaches a high level in militant societies. Loyalty and faith in personal agencies are likewise indispensable, and very highly valued. The citizen is regarded as the property of the State, which regulates his life down to small details. There is great rigidity in the body politic, and obstacles in the way of changing social position, occupation, or locality. There is a tendency for the State to do everything, and for the consequent suppression of private organisations. The militant society tends to be self-supporting; for its constant hostility to surrounding societies requires it to produce for itself all that it needs. Protection is a natural result of this policy.

Various civilised and uncivilised peoples are named as illustrating the militant type. Among modern civilised societies Russia is especially referred to. Wars invariably tend to strengthen the military type, and peace to weaken it. In illustration of this truth Germany is cited; and attention is drawn to the rapid growth of militarism in many different spheres of political life as a result of her wars. The same tendency is noted in England.

The industrial type of society presents a strong contrast to the militant type. An accurate description of it is hindered by the fact that all modern societies are to some extent militant,

and it is not possible, therefore, to exemplify
the characters of a purely industrial State. The
type to which the most industrial and least militant States tend, however, is as follows :—Corpo-
rate activity by the State as a whole is much less
conspicuous. A despotic government is absolutely
excluded. A high degree of individual liberty is
reached—complete liberty, indeed, limited only by
the prohibition of aggression on others. Such
orders as are issued, or laws as are passed, are
negative rather than positive : they prohibit
certain actions by citizens, but do not lay upon
the citizens any injunctions for positive action.
Government is on the representative principle,
but its functions are practically reduced to the
maintenance of order and justice. There is no
state charity or artificial distribution of benefits :
there is, on the other hand, a very wide extension
of private organisations for carrying on much
work which in semi-militant societies is often in
the hands of the Government. The *régime* of
status is replaced entirely by the *régime* of contract,
compulsory co-operation by voluntary co-operation. Resulting from these features, the industrial
State shows a relative plasticity, determined by
the principle that the efficient win the rewards
of life. A further tendency is towards the dissolution of the idea of nationality—freedom of trade
between nations leading to a more or less common

organisation running through them all. It is shown how nations in modern times have advanced towards this ideal from their more militant condition in mediæval times.

It has already been observed that the constitution of any society is a function of the characters of the individuals composing it. Hence we must expect to find militant societies composed of persons of quite different natures from those typical of industrial societies. The typical member of a militant society identifies virtue with bravery and strength : he regards revenge, especially in public matters, as a duty ; and the deadening of sympathies consequent upon war produces a state of selfishness in peace. Patriotism and loyalty are powerful sentiments in such a man. Obedience is regarded as one of the highest virtues. Faith in authority engenders a low development of initiative, and an abundant belief in the extension of official control.

The typical member of an industrial society, on the other hand, is characterised by wholly different qualities. He is devoid of feelings of revenge, and he is full of humane sentiment, causing him to respect the rights of others. He is extremely independent and has a high regard for personal liberty. His loyalty and patriotism are less marked : he has little faith in authority, but is of enterprising and inquiring disposition.

After dealing with the militant and industrial types of society, we at length reach the close of " Political Institutions " which terminates with a speculation as to the future political condition if societies continue to evolve to their highest stage.   According to this speculation, the office of head of the State will decline in importance and will be filled by election.   Government will be carried on perhaps by one or two Chambers elected in one way or otner.   The *form* of government is likely to vary, while the *substance* is not.   Under any political form State functions will be brought within extremely narrow limits—the maintenance of justice and internal order.   The other functions now carried on by Government will be taken over by private organisations, which will be far more numerous and extensive than at present.   But above all, and far more important than all, is the cessation of war.   Only through permanent peace can the highest social evolution be attained ; and every outbreak of war sets back the progress and improvement of political institutions.   On this theme, the second volume of " The Principles of Sociology " comes to an end.

Yet we cannot feel that the propositions formulated are altogether beyond criticism.   Spencer attempts no analysis of the general causes of war and militancy ; nor does he make any reference to that deep instinct in human nature which causes warfare periodically to break out. Subsequent progress makes it appear doubtful whether the industrial *régime* is really accompanied with all the virtues attributed to it by Spencer. The facts with which we have to deal are complex to the last degree : the thread of principle which Spencer runs through them seems too simple and elementary to unite them all in one. His method may perhaps once again be impugned : a superficial survey of the customs of primitive peoples is scarcely an adequate foundation for so large a generalisation More psychological analysis is needed ; and probably our knowledge of psychology is yet insufficient. Everywhere Spencer's anti-military bias is apparent ; and, however strongly we may share that bias, we must attempt rigidly to exclude it from influencing our speculations. When all his theories are in strong support of the sentiments with which we know he originally set out, our suspicions are inevitably excited. Probably our most scientific attitude in the present state of knowledge is to confess that the whole subject is as yet insufficiently illuminated to enable us to draw any very certain conclusions at all.

" ECCLESIASTICAL INSTITUTIONS."

The third volume of " The Principles of Sociology " opens with an account of " Ecclesiastical Institutions." The ghost theory is once

again recapitulated ; and special emphasis is laid
on the proposition that if all forms of religious
worship are derived from the propitiation of
deceased ancestors, the same must hold good
with regard to that form which is embodied in
Christianity. The Jahveh of the Old Testament
means " the strong one "—" a man of war."
Originally a local potentate, he came to be worshipped after his death as one of the most powerful
spirits of past chiefs.

As soon as the belief in spirits and gods becomes
established, there springs up a class of men whose
duty it is to act as intermediary between them
and people still living. This class is that of the
medicine-men and priests. The medicine-men
deal with spirits by antagonistic measures, such
as exorcism, etc. ; the priests by propitiatory
measures. The medicine-man frightens away or
deceives the spirit by various ruses ; the priest
worships and persuades. With the death of a
chief or head of a family the duty of propitiating
his ghost and attending to its supposed wants
devolves upon his descendants, and especially
upon his eldest male descendant. It thus happens
that in primitive times the ruler and the priest are
combined in one individual. As the ruler becomes
more powerful, and his duties more numerous, he is
compelled to delegate many of his functions, and he
appoints, Spencer continues, some other member of

his family to propitiate his departed ancestry. As families and societies become welded together to form larger groups, a great number of gods are recognised by the various sections of each group ; and an ecclesiastical class is constituted out of those who have been specially delegated to the service of these gods. The state of polytheism thus arising will by various natural processes develop towards monotheism. One of the gods worshipped acquires a gradual ascendancy over the rest ; and his adherents include an increasing proportion of the community, some of whom perhaps have been dissatisfied with the assistance received from their own private gods.

An ecclesiastical organisation, once formed, develops on lines similar to the political organisation—the one being supported by reverence for the dead, and the other by reverence for the living. Monasticism takes a place also in ecclesiastical institutions. The habit of giving clothes and all sorts of goods in propitiation of the dead generates the custom of asceticism. For these donations involve discomfort to the giver : discomfort comes, therefore, to be associated with sanctity, and to be pursued for its own sake. On this thesis it may be remarked that modern inquiries seem to indicate a much deeper organic cause for asceticism. Spencer's perennial search for a logical origin blinds him to the truth that the origin is psychological.

Ecclesiastical institutions, he goes on, have gone hand in hand with political institutions in advancing social integration. For they have supplied a further incentive to obedience and self-restraint, which have facilitated that compulsory co-operation which is a necessary discipline on the way to voluntary co-operation. The priest class have, moreover, commonly furthered military activities, and thus assisted in social evolution in the past. At first the Church and State are one. By degrees they begin to be differentiated ; and where the belief in the supernatural is strong the Church becomes predominant. With the rise of industrialism and a resulting decline of belief in the supernatural, however, the main power passes to the State, and the Church becomes subordinate. The same cause, producing a dislike of authority, leads at last to Nonconformity of various kinds, and to a demand for Disestablishment. The essence of Nonconformity is rebellion against the authority of the priesthood.

From the moral point of view, Spencer asserts that the priesthood has been useful in the past by fostering the spirit of conservatism in social arrangements—by inculcating obedience and by assisting the *régime* of coercion. These advantages, however, gradually cease with the industrialisation of society.

For a system of ethics then arises that is independent of a theological foundation : the priests nevertheless continue to impress moral laws, not because they are intrinsically moral, but as a matter of obedience to authority. And thus they are in various respects inimical to true morality, especially in their tendency to foster the revengeful and military spirit of humanity.

Looking to the future of ecclesiastical institutions, we are not to suppose that they will entirely disappear, although they are likely to alter very widely that sacerdotal element which they now exhibit. It is probable, however, that meetings will continue to be held among the people for the purpose, not of worship, but of contemplating the mysteries of the Unknown Power at the back of the universe. Such contemplation may be carried out to the accompaniment of music, and will serve to take men out of the material routine of their daily lives. Sermons may also be delivered dealing with the proper conduct of life in all its branches, but those who act as ministers will be completely devoid of any sacerdotal character.

Passing from the ecclesiastical prospect to the religious prospect, Spencer anticipates that the idea of a God will lose all its anthropomorphic characters, until nothing remains but a belief in an Unknowable Power which is the cause and origin of the universe and all things in it. It does not follow that because more primitive ideas of a deity are false therefore the highly refined belief in an Unknowable First Cause is also false. On the contrary, it is the germ of truth which has run through and found expression in all forms of religion. Science, says Spencer, does not dissipate religious beliefs; for it confirms and places on a footing of the highest certainty the truth that we are " in presence of an Infinite and Eternal Energy, from which all things proceed." [1]

" PROFESSIONAL INSTITUTIONS."

The next division of " The Principles of Sociology " is occupied with " Professional Institutions." The various groups of institutions hitherto dealt with are concerned with the security or regulation of social life. The professions, on the other hand, are concerned with the *augmentation* of social life; they are directed towards the enhancement of the value and fulness of life. All the professional institutions have evolved in course of time from ecclesiastical institutions, however widely different many of them may now appear. Spencer proceeds to consider the origin and development of each one in turn.

The physician is descended from the medicine-man of primitive communities; and, as already pointed out, the medicine-man and the priest are

[1] This doctrine is criticised in Chapter VIII., dealing with Spencer's Metaphysics.

originally one. The primitive belief about diseases is that they are due to an evil spirit, or possession by a devil; and the means for curing diseases depend upon driving away the spirit. Hence the medicine-man resorts to procedure for the purpose of making the spirit uncomfortable in its human habitat, by thrashing or scorching the patient, etc., or by giving him foul drugs—" dung of elephant, the left foot of a tortoise, liver of a mole, powdered excrement of rats, etc." Even in our own day there survives a belief in an association between the curative powers of a medicine and the nastiness of its taste. Barber-surgeons grew up at a much later date, and were secular long before the physicians became secular. The idea was that surgeons dealt with those injuries that were naturally caused and physicians with those that were supernaturally caused.

The next profession dealt with is that of dancer and musician. When the chief of a savage tribe returns from a successful war his joyful people come forth to meet him; and their emotions find vent in saltatory and vocal activities : here we find the germ of dancing and music. From being practised before the living ruler, they come to be practised before the deceased ruler or god, and thus acquire an ecclesiastical significance. After a time a special group of priests would become differentiated for this purpose and acquire special

skill.   Singing and dancing, at first practised
together, would also become differentiated and a
special class formed for the conduct of each.
By degrees these professions would become secularised instead of being limited to religious
matters.

Orator and poet, actor and dramatist, have
similar beginnings. They all arise, according to
Spencer, from a single origin in the man who re-
counts the deeds of departed warriors and utters
eulogies on their ghosts. His record of heroic
achievements would often be accompanied with
mimicry of their various exploits. With gradual
evolution the orator and actor, the poet and
dramatist, become differentiated from one another
and lose the marks of their religious origin. The
biographer, historian, and man of letters obviously
originate from the same germ : fiction develops
at a later period from biography ; and all these
professions become secularised.

The medicine-man who has to exorcise diseases
naturally seizes any opportunity of acquiring
knowledge which may help him in his art. He
alone has the necessary leisure and opportunity
for acquiring such knowledge. Hence arise the
philosopher and man of science—the one studying
abstract, and the other concrete knowledge.
These professions similarly become secularised,
and, indeed, ultimately come into opposition with

their ecclesiastical parentage. As the priests are the possessors of knowledge, they become likewise the teachers of youth ; and the relation between parson and schoolmaster still subsists to some degree among ourselves. They also become the arbiters of law ; for in its origin law was the supposed commands of the ghosts of the dead. The different occupations of judges, lawyers, etc., become gradually distinct as law slowly ceases to be ecclesiastical.

The architect, says Spencer, likewise originated from the priest. Mounds, temples, etc., were erected over the bodies of the dead, either to ensure their preservation from accidents, or as a mark of honour. Architecture, beginning in this way, slowly became secularised like the other professions, and now occupies the energies of a specialised class. But even earlier than the origin of architecture, it was customary to make effigies of the dead, into which their ghosts might enter if they should feel disposed, and which, consequently, often served as idols. From the manufacture of these effigies sculpture was developed. In order to give the effigy a more realistic appearance, it was commonly painted ; and it was only by degrees that sculpture and painting were separated and developed into two different arts. The ancient cave paintings found in various countries are *not* the ancestry of modern painting, which, on the contrary, has, in Spencer's opinion, a purely ecclesiastical origin.

Although painting was therefore limited at first to figures, a period arose when several figures were represented together with a landscape as a background. By degrees the lansdcape began to be painted for its own sake, though it is only in modern times that the figures have been altogether dropped out. Even now it is common to include representations of living animals.

Regarding the evolution of the professions as a whole, Spencer points out how they conform to the main law of evolution established in " First Principles." From an indefinite homogeneity they gradually attain a definite heterogeneity. They were at first confused together—painting with sculpture, music with dancing, oratory with poetry and drama, etc. ; and all of them were practised by the priest. But ultimately each becomes sharply differentiated from the rest and forms the occupation of a special class.

From this study we should learn how social evolution is achieved without conscious purpose, but purely through the pursuit by each individual of what he conceives to be his own interests. Practically the whole organisation of society has arisen as a result of the pursuit by citizens of their own private ends. Yet politicians systematically ignore this immensely significant truth ; they think that social evolution may be turned this way or that by merely passing laws, ordering people to do what they imagine ought to be done : they insist upon the superstition that society may be manufactured by carefully arranged measures, and will not recognise that it is a natural growth. Social schemers remain blind to the plainest lessons of sociological inquiries.

" INDUSTRIAL INSTITUTIONS."

After drawing this moral, Spencer passes to the final division of " The Principles of Sociology," dealing with " Industrial Institutions." In an introductory chapter it is pointed out that social evolution, which at first moves exceedingly slowly, gradually advances with increasing velocity. " The power of the evolving influences augments in a duplicate ratio, the power of the opposing influences diminishes in a duplicate ratio " . . . " until at length the speed has become such that the improvements which science and enterprise have achieved during this [last] century, are greater in amount than those achieved during all past centuries put together."

The main features of division of labour are next described. The earliest and most natural form of division of labour was that between the two sexes. Division of labour is either topical, local, or detailed. " Topical " refers to division of labour between different localities—as, for instance, cutlery at Sheffield, cotton-spinning at Oldham, etc. Local division of labour is that division which takes place within the same locality ; and the "detailed" division refers to the small specialisations within a single establishment. Division of labour is also simultaneous and successive : a single product may, for instance, be passed through a succession of different processes, or it may be combined with other products simultaneously manufactured.

In social evolution property is first obtained by acquisition or conquest of others. Production by labour gradually supersedes acquisition ; for without production there is only a narrow range of objects worth the trouble of acquisition. The production is at first directed towards satisfaction of the strongest needs. Originally purely manual, it passes after a time into the stage of domestic animals ; and with higher civilisation this stage again gives place to the era of machinery.

Production and distribution in early times were not distinct. The man who had made an article himself got into touch with another man who required it ; and a common means for effecting the transference was through the agency of fairs. Exchange was a form of barter ; and barter, as already described, arose from the habit of giving presents for propitiatory purposes. Money was

introduced at a much later stage. It was introduced in various different forms : cattle were used
very commonly for the purposes of money (whence
the term " impecunious "). In more recent times
" promises to pay " written on paper have to a
large extent taken the place of metallic money ;
and there has been in effect a resumption of a
form of barter—where goods only are exchanged,
and the financial transaction is limited to entries
in account-books, the two sides of which generally
balance.

The interdependence and integration of industrial institutions with advancing evolution are
next considered. The production of any article
requires the co-operation of many different appliances in one machine, and often of various different
machines. In the manufacture of newspapers,
for instance, one machine has to manufacture the
paper, another prints upon it, while others again
cut it into separate sheets and fold it up. It is not
usual to make the paper at the same place where
the printing is done ; but, in the absence of
impediments, it might be arranged that at one end
of the united machines there was supplied a stream
of wet pulp, while at the other there were delivered
the printed and folded newspapers.

The evolution of this complicated system of
industrial interdependence without any conscious
purpose, but purely through the pursuit by

citizens of their private ends, furnishes another
opportunity for criticism of the social schemer,
who imagines that industrial evolution is the result
of direct governmental interposition. "A fly
seated on the surface of the body has about as
good a conception of its internal structure as one
of these schemers has of the social organisation in
which he is imbedded."

Dealing next with the regulation of labour, it
is shown that coercive industrial regulation is
allied to coercive political regulation. Where the
greatest freedom has been attained in political
institutions, there is least interference with labour
and industrial institutions. Passing to slavery,
it is shown that this form of compulsory labour is
very general among all races, and that it is proper
to communities which live in a constant state of
war. Trade unionism is considered : the benefits
which it has brought are recognised, but the
tyranny which it is now so ready to exercise is
warmly condemned. Co-operation is then dealt
with—the conclusion reached being that, though
excellent in principle, it demands a higher type of
human nature than is at all common at the present
time. Success, therefore, is only likely to be
achieved where the co-operative community is
very select.

Socialism is biologically fatal and psychologically absurd. Under the normal and healthy

system, rewards are apportioned to deserts : the inefficient are poorly provided for. If, however, a Socialistic arrangement rewards people according to their *needs* and not according to their *merits*, it follows that the least efficient part of the community will be able to multiply like the rest, leading in course of time to a society composed of inefficients. Socialism, moreover, is psychologically absurd in its assumption that men will work as hard in the abstract interests of the community as they will in pursuance of their own interests.

An attempt is next made to prophesy the course of public affairs in the near future. The result of the inquiries embodied in " The Principles of Sociology " shows that the most fundamental differences between societies are those which depend upon the relative positions of the individual and the State. In recent European history there was manifest a continual encroachment of the State upon the freedom of the individual. This encroachment, Spencer continues, took two forms—the first, military, typified by France and Germany with their systems of conscription, and the enormous taxation in those as well as in our own country for the maintenance of military armaments ; the second, Socialistic, likewise far more prominent in France and Germany than in Great Britain. Militarism and Socialism are two aspects of the same spirit : they both imply

compulsory instead of voluntary co-operation,
though they aim at different results. The further
growth of the military and communistic spirits
are foreshadowed in the near future. Recollecting
the doctrine of the rhythm of motion established
in " First Principles," we cannot expect that
social evolution will continue smoothly along its
destined path. It proceeds rather by a succession
of steps forward, with many retrogressive steps
intervening. After centuries of decline in coercive
rule, there was reached in the middle of last century in England " a degree of individual freedom
greater than ever before existed since nations began
to be formed. Men could move about as they
pleased, work at what they pleased, trade with
whom they pleased." A return movement, however, had set in ; freedom was diminished every
year by new legislation, and by the ever-increasing
burdens of armaments. But the reaction, however long it may last, will ultimately give way to
a renewed period of progress, and to the attainment
of a more perfect freedom, in proportion as human
nature itself becomes more perfect. " The ultimate man will be one whose private requirements
coincide with public ones. He will be that manner
of man who, in spontaneously fulfilling his own
nature, incidentally performs the functions of a
social unit ; and yet is only enabled so to fulfil
his own nature by all others doing the like."

CHAPTER VII

GENERAL SUMMARY OF "THE PRINCIPLES OF ETHICS"

WE now reach the final division of the Synthetic Philosophy, and that division which was regarded by Spencer himself as the most important part of the whole undertaking. It opens, in consonance with the general plan of the Philosophy, with a part on "The Data of Ethics."

"THE DATA OF ETHICS."

It is clear from the beginning that only a certain part of human conduct has any ethical or moral colouring, and that very many of the activities of mankind are neither moral nor immoral, and therefore do not fall within the scope of Ethics. Taking the activities of animals as a whole, it is found that they may be divided into the two classes of those which have and those which have not a purpose ; and the higher we climb up the scale of evolution the more do the purposive activities of animals predominate over the unpurposive. A low organism swims or floats about at random in the water, and depends for its food on the chance contact of suitable materials. A higher animal adopts definite activities for the purpose of obtaining food ; its movements are guided far more by direct reference to the end in view. It is this purposive kind of activity only that is comprised within the name of conduct ; and the improvement of conduct is nothing else than the better adjustment of means to end.

Evolution of conduct therefore implies, according to Spencer, a progress in those kinds of activities which favour the preservation of life. There are three different ends to which the activities may be directed : life of the individual, as in the instance above-named, life of the species, as illustrated by care of offspring, etc. ; and lastly social life, avoidance of anything that may conflict with the lives of others, and furtherance of anything that may promote their lives. Good conduct is that in which these ends are achieved to a high extent ; bad conduct that in which they fall short to a greater or lesser degree from the requirements. The essence of high morality, then, is in the preservation of life ; and that conduct is most moral which conduces most to this preservation, and which therefore is most evolved. Ethics is based on evolution.

The preservation of life is only desirable, Spencer continues, on the assumption that life brings in its train more happiness than unhappiness. The attainment of happiness is the end of life ; and this doctrine is one which cannot be denied even by ascetics, who practise severities and suffer hardships in the present life with a view to achieving greater happiness in a future life. While, therefore, the purpose of an ethical system is the preservation of life, it is also the attainment of happiness. Our Ethics is both evolutionary and hedonistic. Nor is there any opposition between these two ends. Happiness furthers the ends of life in a great variety of ways ; and pain, as such, is a falling-short from the fullness of life and a symptom of inadequate preservation.

As in so many parts of Spencer's social writings this particular theory seems to pay inadequate attention to psychological analysis. No one proclaimed so emphatically as Spencer that sociology is dependent upon psychology ; but time after time his sociological theories suffer from the imperfections of the psychology of his time. Spencer's Ethics is based on hedonism, a doctrine much in vogue among the advanced thinkers of last century, but now comparatively discredited, not only in Ethics, but in political economy and the other branches of philosophy where it was commonly applied. From the *à priori* point of view, it would indeed appear eminently reasonable to assert that the activities of men are guided by their desire to procure happiness, and to escape unhappiness. But actual observation of mankind quickly dispels this naïve supposition. Spencer never took note of what are called *idées fixes*,

which constitute the true motives of a large part
of human activity. A particular idea or suggestion
once grafted on to the mind tends to work itself
out in conduct, altogether independently of any
reasonable estimate of happiness or unhappiness,
and with disastrous consequences to all theories
of hedonism, or to the cognate doctrine of utilitarianism. The true way of inducing mankind or
a single man to pursue a certain line of activity
is *not* by appealing to intellectual considerations
of the happiness which will ensue to him there-
from, but by impressing the idea of that line of
activity upon his mind. Suggestion is in any
sphere a more potent motive than hedonism.
Spencer is unquestionably wrong in attributing
the conduct of ascetics to an anticipation of
pleasure in a future life. There are in existence at
the present day many persons who harbour no
such anticipations, and who yet lead lives that are
ascetic in many minor ways. Habit, social convention, suggestion, are the instruments at work.
The domination of some particular idea is the all-
sufficient motive in accounting for conduct, and the
question as to how that domination occurred is to
a great extent irrelevant. It is as much a part of
the man's consitution as the shape of his nose.
As already insisted, the explanation of human
conduct and belief belongs to Psychology, and not,
as Spencer persistently assumed, to Logic. Man

is primarily a being of emotions and feelings ; and in that region we must seek explanations of his behaviour. He is only secondarily an intellectual being ; but his intellect and knowledge are exceedingly superficial biologically, and of very late appearance in evolution. They are not rooted in his constitution, as are his emotions ; and they are of incomparably less weight in determining either his beliefs or his conduct.

Spencer next passes to consider morals from several different points of view—the physical, the biological, the psychological, and the sociological. From the physical point of view high moral conduct (he says) is that which answers most closely to the definition of evolution given in "First Principles." It is characterised by definiteness, coherence, and heterogeneity. The adjustment of acts to ends is definite in the sense that they are precisely adapted to the achievement of those ends. Appointments are punctually kept, statements made are strictly accurate, work done is not slipshod, etc. Coherence is manifested in the steadiness of purpose, which combines a variety of actions to the consummation of the end in view. And heterogeneity is displayed in the wide range of methods by which different ends are reached. The conduct of a highly moral man embraces a wide variety of actions, in addition to its definiteness and coherence or singleness of purpose.

From the biological point of view, Spencer argues that pleasure is the normal concomitant of life-conserving activities, and pain of life-destroying activities. Had it been otherwise, evolution would quickly have ended; for animals in general necessarily pass their lives in avoiding pain and seeking gratifications, and if this kind of conduct had not been conducive to preservation of life, species would quickly have become extinct. In the case of men, however, the immediate relation between pleasure and the maintenance of life is to some extent abrogated. As mankind are passing from a state of separation and independence to a higher social state, their lives are largely artificial. They are as yet imperfectly adapted to social life; and their feelings are not a true guide to the kind of conduct which social life demands. Nevertheless the school of thought which glorifies pain and depreciates pleasure is in fundamental error; for pleasure and pain constitute a true index to conduct in a large number of cases, and will become still more reliable as guides in proportion as humanity progresses.

From the psychological view, it is pointed out that the pleasure derived from the higher emotions is a more correct guide than that derived from the lower. Spencer infers that the essential trait of a moral consciousness is the subordination of one feeling by another. It is obvious that many advantages arise from the suppression of an immediate feeling by another which interdicts it : by the sacrifice of immediate pleasures it continually happens that greater and more enduring ultimate pleasures are attained. From observation of this fact by primitive peoples a moral consciousness gradually developed, which urged the postponement of present gratification to future happiness ; and it is from this origin that Spencer believed the moral consciousness had sprung.

Once again comment must be made on the astonishing conception which Spencer has of primitive man forming generalisations in Ethics, based upon extensive and difficult observations of what is and what is not good for society at large. The conception is almost as elementary as that of the " social contract " by Hobbes and Rousseau. It credits primitive men, not only with being philosophers, but with being philosophers of most remarkable powers and knowledge. It credits also successive generations with the maintenance of the philosophy of their brilliant ancestors. Probably we may find here evidence of the working of one of Spencer's biological fallacies. He assumes in " The Data of Ethics," as in many other parts of his Philosophy, that acquired characters are inherited. He imagines that if during several successive generations a particular code of morals is taught to men, that code will become congenital. The theory is now discredited, and the conclusion drawn from it is palpably false. Moral codes do not engender moral sentiments, but *vice versâ*. The moral sentiments are truly congenital ; they call into existence moral codes in harmony with them, and these of course can be handed down by tradition from generation to generation, but never become congenital in the true sense. If we must seek an explanation in Biology, we shall find it far more readily in Natural Selection than in the antique theory of use-inheritance. Tribes which possess a congenital moral sentiment can hold together in societies ; and by the strength of their union they survive. Tribes, on the other hand, which lack a moral sentiment are quickly disintegrated and broken up. In the struggle for existence, they are soon squeezed out by the strength of the naturally more moral races. How, then, do the moral sentiments arise ? The answer to that question may wait till biologists have informed us how variations arise. At present nothing whatever is known upon the subject. All that we can see is that in the earliest ages of the history of man some fortunate variation brought into existence a race with some sort of moral sentiment. Immediately union and social life became possible : henceforward that race was destined to multiply at the expense of the less fortunate part of mankind which had not undergone the variation. It is quite plain that the surviving races must be those whose instincts are social, or moral. Those whose instincts are anti-social are weak by virtue of their inability to unite : they are doomed to extinction, and in fact are extinguished as soon as they come in contact with a more social race.

Spencer next passes from what he calls the psychological point of view to the sociological point of view. He points out that in primitive societies, constantly at war, the State must take precedence of the individual. But as hostile States cease to constitute a danger, the welfare of individuals becomes the object to be attained ; for the State, as a State, has no feeling, and its welfare is a matter of indifference, except as it may influence the welfare of its citizens. As war gradually declines with increasing civilisation, a compromise is reached between the priority of the State, adapted to war, and the priority of the individual, adapted to peace. When at length permanent peace is secured, there will be no restraint placed upon individuals, except such as may be necessary for the prevention of direct aggression, or of breach of contract.

After insisting upon the relativity of pains and pleasures—and the varying sentiments of mankind towards them—Spencer proceeds to a general discussion of egoism and altruism. The importance of a rational egoism is set forth; for without proper regard for self there is no power of subserving the needs of others. But altruism is likewise of the highest importance for social life. Though at first it has to be carefully cultivated and enforced, human nature is gradually advancing into more complete harmony with social life: eventually there will no longer be any need for impressing altruism, since citizens will of their own accord desire the welfare of others and derive satisfaction from the furtherance of it. Utilitarianism errs in emphasising altruism at the expense of egoism. The wants of each citizen, being to a certain extent individual and peculiar to himself, are more easily satisfied by his own action than by the action of others. If, therefore, everyone were to abandon the pursuit of his own happiness, and give up his time to promoting the happiness of others, the result would be a smaller general happiness than might be. For each citizen would have his needs fulfilled less perfectly than if he himself had attended to them. The true course, therefore, is a rational egoism, modified by altruism. Each citizen should be free to pursue his own ends, so long as the similar freedom of other citizens is not interfered with.

The contrast is noted between Absolute and Relative Ethics. Absolute Ethics assumes that individuals have already reached a state of moral perfection ; and a true system of Absolute Ethics is that which would prevail among a race of perfect men. Where men are imperfect, their relations are not capable of being formulated within any system, any more than there could be a geometry where the lines drawn were crooked and arbitrary. All that can now be attained, therefore, is a Relative Ethics : in many situations there is no absolutely right course, but there is perhaps one which, though not perfect, is relatively better than any other. Any system of Ethics on a scientific basis must be an Absolute system ; and its use in practical life is that we may select those lines of conduct which come nearest to its complete fulfilment.

The subject of Ethics falls into various departments. First comes the Ethics of Individual Life ; then Justice ; then Beneficence, positive and negative. The most important division of Ethics is that dealing with Justice ; for here is described the system of relationships between individuals which should be maintained by the authority of the State. We pass now from " The Data of Ethics " to these various departments ; but before dealing with them we have to take a general view of " The Inductions of Ethics."

"The Inductions of Ethics."

The main thesis of this part is that civilised mankind have two opposing systems of morality : the religion of amity and the religion of enmity. The former—namely, Christianity—is their ostensible religion, but the latter is their true religion. It is illustrated by the feelings of antagonism existing between different nations, by the conquest of smaller and less civilised nations by the larger and more powerful, by duelling in countries which still retain that institution, and by the accompanying code of honour, which inculcates the principle of revenge in opposition to the religion of amity. An instance is given of barbaric and militaristic religion in a general order issued to his soldiers by the present Kaiser of Germany on his ascent to the throne : " God's decree places me at the head of the Army " ; and then, after expressing his submission to " God's will," he goes on to swear " ever to remember that the eyes of my ancestors look down upon me from the other world, and that I shall one day have to render account to them of the glory and honour of the army."

Thus the sentiments of mankind are not truly ethical, but pro-ethical : they are sentiments which fill the place of genuine moral sentiments. History, consisting largely of a record of wars and battles, "is little more than the Newgate Calendar of nations."

The remainder of "The Inductions of Ethics" is taken up by a consideration of each of the ordinarily recognised virtues in turn, and an attempt to affiliate them with one or other kind of social type, especially the military and industrial types. Aggression and robbery are found to be most marked in military States. Being accustomed by training to force and violence, such States are naturally prone to commit corresponding crimes against other States, and their individuals to commit them against one another. Revenge is equally characteristic of military communities : but from primitive forms of revenge grows Justice ; and Justice prevails in proportion to the peacefulness and industrial development of society. Generosity and Humanity are likewise developed in inverse proportion to the warlike qualities of the people. Truthfulness has a somewhat less direct connection ; for the Hottentots are an eminently veracious people, though they have not infrequent wars. Their mode of government is singularly free from coerciveness ; this and many other facts lead Spencer to the conclusion that the prevalence of truthfulness is directly proportioned to freedom, and that it is least in those communities which have the most coercive rule. As these are generally military communities, there is an indirect relation between unveracity and war. Complete truthfulness is very rare ; for even in ordinary speech it is common to exaggerate, and to make use of words like " very " on occasions when they are not called for.

Obedience has a double character. On the one hand, filial obedience is rooted in Nature, and has a high ethical warrant ; but other kinds of obedience, that for instance to authority and to government, is pro-ethical. It exists most strongly in militant societies ; and with the advance of pacific qualities it ceases to be a virtue and gives way to the only ethical obedience, namely, obedience to one's own conscience.

Industry is least in military States, where labour is usually despised and left to the women and the slaves. As peace becomes more permanent, industry becomes honourable. Temperance, on the other hand, appears to exhibit no relationship to any one social type ; it is rapidly increasing at the present time. Chastity is also difficult to classify. Unchastity appears to be specially characteristic of military States ; but it cannot be said that chastity is characteristic of peaceful States. The evil caused by unchastity is an ultimate lowering of the population in number or quality.

The conclusion established by " The Inductions of Ethics " is that war is the root of nearly all social evil. Just as many savage tribes are cannibals or anthropophagous, so our existing communities of Europe are "sociophagous." "There needs but a continuance of absolute peace externally and a rigorous insistence on non-aggression internally, to ensure the moulding of men into a form naturally characterised by all the virtues."

Here Spencer commits himself in a more specific form to the fallacy of his Biology, that acquired characters are inherited. He imagines that men can be "moulded" by their environment; that peace and justice produce a certain effect on character, and that that effect will be inherited. This latter opinion, however widely it may be held by popular ignorance, is untrue. No alteration or improvement of environment can produce any direct action on the congenital qualities of men. It may, of course, elevate the characters of each successive generation in turn : but the improvement does not show even a disposition to be inherited ; human character is not touched by it ; no improvement of conditions can "mould" the hereditary qualities of mankind ; nor can any deterioration of those conditions degrade his hereditary qualities, except, indeed, by the indirect method of causing extinction of the best strains and multiplication of the worst.

"THE ETHICS OF INDIVIDUAL LIFE."

Leaving now " The Inductions of Ethics," we reach part iii., dealing with " The Ethics of Individual Life." The doctrine is laid down that the moral sphere is wider than commonly supposed, and that it includes much of the conduct which is of purely personal concern. More especially the pursuit of healthy gratifications is enjoined, and the belief that all pleasure is evil or indifferent is emphatically condemned. Anything which brings individual gratification, without injury either to self or others, is physiologically wholesome, in that it leads to a more efficient and therefore better life.

A proper physical activity should be maintained. Idleness is to be reprobated ; but so also is over-work. It is imperative, Spencer continues, that a due amount of rest should be taken, though many people sleep too long and reduce their efficiency in consequence. So also do others eat too much, causing injury to themselves and waste to the community ; yet variety of food and attention to the demands of the palate are ethically right as aiding digestion and a more perfect life. Alcoholic stimulation is from the point of view of Absolute Ethics entirely reprehensible ; but in the present imperfect condition of mankind the consumption of alcohol by adults is often to be regarded as relatively

right. The pursuit of culture is a true ethical
aim ; it should be culture not only of the mind
but of the body, in so far as the acquirement of
manual dexterity is concerned : intellectual culture
is chiefly given by the study of science.

Amusements constitute a further object of
ethical sanction. Reading novels and going to
theatres is right, so long as it is not overdone,
and so long as the books or plays selected are
of a humanising and not a brutalising character.
Music is especially deserving of praise. Passing
to the active amusements, all sport is condemned
by Spencer, in that it inflicts pain on other
creatures and thus sears the sympathies. Foot-
ball is reprehensible for the same reason ; and
some indoor games, such as chess, is so (to a much
less extent) because of the humiliation entailed
upon the loser in a game of so purely an intellectual
character. This objection is removed in games
of chance ; though all forms of betting and
gambling are condemned for the reason that the
pleasure of the victor is attained by the pain of
the loser. The same objection is raised to various
forms of outdoor games, such as boat-racing.
On these opinions I have already made some
criticism in a previous chapter.

Marriage and parentage are next dealt with.
Very early marriages are to be reprobated on
physiological grounds ; and so also is the so-called

mariage de convenance. The responsibilities of parentage are emphasised, and condemnation is expressed of all social legislation which tends to relieve parents of the care and responsibility of their children, not excluding even their education.

We have now reached the end of " The Ethics of Individual Life." It represents really a protest against the somewhat ascetic notions of morality widely held in Spencer's time. In so far it was no doubt useful; but we may be of the opinion that he travelled too far in the opposite direction. We may disagree with him altogether in extending the sphere of morality to cover so many details of private life. Take, for example, one of Spencer's favourite illustrations. He condemned the puritanical objections which were often raised in his time to playing a game such as billiards. Personally he liked billiards, and he thought it incumbent on him to prove that it was in conformity with ethical principles. But nowadays Ethics does not intrude in these minor affairs of life. In such matters moral maxims no longer enter. We laugh at the Puritan (if he still exists) and continue to play. Generally speaking, Ethics, like laws, may be greatly overdone. If moral principles are operative in every detail of life, we become dogmatic and hidebound, tied up in a network of principles and reduced to the category of prigs. The all-moral man is neither charitable, nor tolerant, nor moral; in straining after gnats he will swallow a camel. For when everything presents itself as a question of right and wrong he loses all sense of moral proportion. The philosophical tendency of the day is to limit rather than increase the sphere of Ethics in individual life; and the tendency has an excellent psychological justification.

We pass now to the second volume of "The Principles of Ethics," dealing with "The Ethics of Social Life"; it opens with the division on "Justice," which was regarded by Spencer as the most important of all his writings.

"JUSTICE."

The roots of the sentiment of Justice are traced by Spencer in the animal world. There the law of natural selection decrees that the less fit shall die out, and that the race shall be carried on from those individuals which are best adapted to their environment. In other words, the law of Nature is that prosperity is apportioned to efficiency; there is a natural relation between survival and competence. Moreover, it is clear that any interference with this relation must be disastrous to the species. For any such interference must mean that the less adapted are enabled to survive and bear offspring, or else that the more adapted are prevented from passing on their better organisations to posterity. In either event the species becomes less well adapted to its environment, and moves a step towards extinction.

Now in human affairs the same law holds good. The strongest men in mind and body—those best adapted for social life—prosper on the average; and, when not interfered with, are enabled to produce and rear offspring of an equally high quality to carry on the race. The weaklings, on the other hand—or at least those less adapted—suffer the penalties of their incompetence, and are unable to rear offspring. The weaker strains die out, and the stronger strains survive. The most important law of social life, therefore, is that which ensures to each man the natural rewards due to his energy and efficiency; and that law is satisfied only by *individual liberty*. There must be no interference with individuals; for interference abrogates the relation between fitness and success.

If human beings were not gregarious, there would be no more to be said; but in social life complete individual freedom must be limited in so far as is necessary to prevent one individual from interfering with the freedom of another. Spencer's law requires that all individuals shall be free, and it seeks to establish the highest sum-total of freedom within the community. For the fulfil-ment of this condition, it is clear that no individual may be permitted to intrench upon the life or liberty of any other individual. Freedom must be equal and universal; and the only restrictions which may be imposed are those required for the maintenance of freedom itself. The formula of Justice therefore contains two clauses, of which the first proclaims the freedom of the individual, and the second supplies the condition that he shall not intrude upon the equal freedom of any other individual. The formula runs as follows: "Every man is free to do that which he wills, provided he infringes not the equal freedom of any other man." The rule of Justice embodied in this formula is the ethical aspect of the law of evolution.

Spencer of course applies the formula only to adults. It is only among adults that natural selection demands the apportionment of benefits to deserts. Among children the opposite holds good; and the most has to be given to the newest infants, whose capacities are least. Among children, benefits are proportioned to incapacity. It is with the former conditions alone that we are concerned in our study of Justice. It is to be noted, moreover, that the formula of Justice belongs to the region of Absolute Ethics, and that in imperfect conditions it cannot be rigidly applied. More particularly its complete application presupposes a condition of permanent peace; for, so long as wars con-

tinue, individual freedom is subject to severe
restrictions, for the purposes of national defence.
Accordingly Spencer finds that in practice the
formula of Justice is most closely realised in those
communities which are most peaceful; and con-
versely that it is farthest from general recognition
in societies of the most militant type.

Spencer thus reached his law of Justice by a
deductive argument: from this law, again, he
deduced the various rights of man; and by
consideration of these in turn he went on to argue
that the development of law had been in the
direction of the continual reinforcement of those
rights which are derived as corollaries from the
formula of Justice.

Firstly we have the right to physical integrity—
that is to say, freedom from all forms of personal
aggression. In accordance with this right, it should
be illegal for a sick person to expose others to
infection, as by travelling in a public conveyance.
Developed law recognises the right to physical
integrity: like all others, however, it is liable to
be suspended in time of war, in the interests of
the community. The rights to free motion and
locomotion are the next corollaries: as in the case
of the former, they are recognised to an increasing
extent by law; but these rights also may properly
be suspended in time of war. The rights to the
uses of natural media justify laws for the prevention

of new buildings which may exclude the light from other habitations ; for the prevention of street noises of disagreeable character, etc. This right would appear also to justify public ownership of the land ; and it does in fact establish a State-suzerainty. The value of the land, however, resides mainly in the cultivation and improvements which have been wrought upon it by individual effort ; and these rightly belong to the individuals who have accomplished them, or who have purchased them with the proceeds of labour earned elsewhere. Whereas the State has, in Spencer's opinion, a right to resume the land if it should wish to do so, such resumption would be impolitic, as the compensation payable to the present owners would be greater than the gain would be worth ; moreover, Spencer finds reason to suppose on general principles that land is administered better by private individuals than by public officials.

The right of property, other than land, is, however, on a different footing ; and the law of Justice prohibits the seizure of property which rightly belongs to individuals who have made or purchased it. The right of incorporeal property is in the same position. The law of copyright should be strengthened : inventors should have proper protection for their ideas, though after a time inventions may rightly become public property. Under the heading of " incorporeal

property " comes also the prohibition of defama-
tion of character—which should be punished,
when the allegations made are untrue.

Next come the rights of gift and bequest, with
certain limitations. Among these limitations is
included the practice of entail. This practice
involves a control by the dead over the property
of the living, and thus constitutes an unjustifiable
interference with liberty. The rights of free
exchange and free contract comprise the doctrine
of free trade, which thus possesses, according to
Spencer, not only an economic but an ethical
sanction. Interference with freedom of trade is a
breach of the formula of Justice ; and protectionists
should therefore be called "aggressionists." The
right to free industry is another obvious corollary
from the formula. The rights of free belief and
worship are similarly beyond the reach of interference, unless they create an uproar which constitutes a public nuisance, as in the case of the
Salvation Army. The rights of free speech and publication are also inviolate, except during wars, when
they may afford useful information to the enemy.
The publication of indecent matter is a difficult
point ; yet there is likely to be greater harm in
legal prohibition than in the circulation of offensive
matter, which is never likely to occur extensively,
and which may safely be left to the power of
public opinion. In the enumeration of these

various rights, which are drawn as corollaries from the formula of Justice, Spencer finds that the evolution of law has always been towards clearer and more definite recognition of them. Conclusions reached *à priori* are thus verified by the actual course of affairs examined *à posteriori*.

Passing now to the rights of women, the formula requires that their freedom shall be equal to those of men. In married life the balance of authority should, Spencer says, be on the side of the husband when agreement cannot be reached ; for men are more judicial and less impulsive than women, and upon men rests the responsibility of finding the means for their joint subsistence. A further difference between men and women is due to the fact that men are liable to military service for the defence of the country in time of war. Since this burden does not fall upon women, they are not entitled to the franchise, until a state of permanent peace has been attained.

After touching on the increasing recognition of the rights of children, we pass to a consideration of rights of altogether different character ; of political rights—so-called. Has every man a right to a vote, and should there be universal franchise ? Propositions such as these cannot be deduced from the law of equal freedom : all that is affirmed by that law is that every man shall be free, so long as he does not infringe the equal freedom of any

other man. The privilege of casting a vote in a
ballot-box is not a right ; and the proper form of
franchise therefore is that which is most likely
to maintain the fundamental law of Ethics. This
is unlikely to be achieved by universal suffrage.
It is a cardinal maxim that men will vote for what
they conceive to be their interest ; legislation is
carried through by conflict of varying interests ;
and it may and does happen that one interest,
which happens to comprise a great many more
individuals than another, would have an unfair
legislative advantage over that other. Our political institutions therefore should be based on
the representation, not of individuals, but of
interests. The actual constitution of the State is
a matter of indifference so long as the law of
equal freedom is maintained.

As to taxation, each man has an equal interest in
the protection of life and liberty ; and equal taxation
should be levied upon all to meet this requirement.
The protection of property, on the other hand,
should be provided for by taxation that is proportioned to the amount of property possessed—
the wealth of the individual. All taxation should
be direct, and should be applied for from each
citizen in a single sum, so that he may know
precisely how much taxation is taken from him in
the course of the year. All indirect taxation or
other methods of collecting money in a way that

is often not perceived by the citizen are condemned as encouraging extravagance.

Coming now to the duties of the State, Spencer held that government originated for the purpose of carrying on war and the defence of the community. The maintenance of internal order was not at first regarded as part of the functions of government ; and this maintenance was only undertaken by Government on the ground that internal dissension was a cause of weakness in the face of the enemy. The functions of government are therefore two in number : the protection of the community from hostile aggression of other communities, and the protection of the individual within the community from the aggression of other individuals—*i.e.*, the maintenance of the rights already enumerated. The protection of the community requires, of course, the maintenance of a navy and army adequate for the purpose. As regards the internal function of the State, Justice should be administered free of cost. Offences would be far less numerous than they are if it was known that reparation could be immediately obtained without expense. Although the State is not directly concerned with the making of railways, roads, etc., yet the alienation of land required for such purposes must be subject to the permission of the State, and their breaking-up or alterations, etc., must be subject to supervision, to ensure that no aggression should be made upon members of the community. In the same way rivers, lakes and inland waters, and the adjacent sea are subject to oversight by the State. These, however, constitute the whole duties of the State. Its functions are, not to make attempts to *further* life, but to maintain intact the *conditions* proper for the natural development of the highest type of life.

From the duties of the State Spencer passes to the further consideration of the limits of those duties. All forms of socialistic legislation or parental government are to be religiously avoided; for they traverse the fundamental law which requires that rewards shall be apportioned to merits. The popular belief that the State may do anything is a superstition: the power of the State should be very sharply restricted. Many instances are adduced of the vices of officialism and the inefficiency of State management, particularly in the departments to which it ought to pay the most exclusive attention. The administration of justice is expensive and slow; the efficiency of the navy and army inadequately watched. If in all departments of industry and business efficiency implies high specialisation, this truth is equally cogent in the sphere of government. A Government which tries to do many things will do them all badly; whereas a Government whose sole attention is devoted to national defence and maintenance of internal justice becomes specialised for those important purposes, and profits by the increased efficiency which follows specialisation.

As was proved in "The Principles of Sociology," Society is a living organism, and not a manufactured product. A society is not made, but grows. A cardinal vice of opportunist legislation is that it is based upon the belief that society may be moulded into one form or other by legislative enactments. Nothing can be farther from the truth: the disappointing effects of such enactments are shown by the enormous proportion of laws which, after being passed, are subsequently repealed. Before their repeal they have been doing harm. So complicated is the structure of the social organism, that the indirect and unforeseen effects of any piece of legislation are commonly far greater and more important than the direct effect which it was hoped to attain. The whole of the wonderful organisation of society, the division of labour, the manufacture of articles in just the right proportion to meet the demands, their transference to the localities where they are most needed, etc., all this organisation has developed without any conscious intention, but purely as an incident in the pursuit by individual men of their personal interests. The daily despatch into London of the food required for the population furnishes an instance. All the different kinds of food arrive in just the right amount to feed the people without waste : they arrive at the right hours in the day. Take for example the case of milk. The supply of milk to London is drawn from innumerable country districts, not bound together by any organisation whatever. Yet it happens that the total amount of the milk sent in from all these country districts is just the exact amount required by the population. And so it is with articles of every kind. If the needs of London were to be provided for by a carefully-devised organisation, it is incredible that the supply should be adapted to the demand with such nicety as it is now, where there is no conscious organisation whatever. In short, the affairs of life are very much better conducted by those natural organisations which grow up without intent to meet the needs of the people than by manufactured organisations which clumsily and stupidly endeavour, at great cost and by compulsory methods, to supply what they imagine to be the needs of the people. With arguments of this character the part dealing with Justice comes to an end.

"The Ethics of Social Life" is divided by Spencer into two main parts, under the titles of "Justice" and "Benevolence." The main practical difference which he draws between the two is that the former may rightly be enforced by law, whereas the latter may not. Although Benevolence should not be a matter for governmental compulsion, it yet constitutes an important branch of Ethics. It occupies the remainder of Spencer's "Principles of Ethics," and is there subdivided into two parts entitled respectively "Negative Beneficence" and "Positive Beneficence."

"NEGATIVE BENEFICENCE."

Dealing first with Negative Beneficence, it is pointed out that the rigour of the social system based upon the enforcement of justice alone may and ought to be tempered by many other restraints which individuals should voluntarily place upon their own actions. Although competition, for example, should be absolutely free as far as the law is concerned, yet competitors ought to observe proper feeling in their relations towards one another. They ought not to lower prices to an unremunerative extent in order to drive others out of the market and then raise them again. A doctor or a lawyer ought not to consider exclusively his own interests, but also the interests of his friends in the profession. On the other hand, trade unions have no right to require that wages paid to the inferior workmen shall be as good as that paid to the superior. A society which acts upon such a plan "will inevitably degenerate and die away in long-drawn miseries."

Negative Beneficence should also set limits upon free contract. It should be held wrong to take advantage of another's misfortunes, to drive an unconscionable bargain with him. The relations between employer and employed should be softened by mutual regard and assistance.

Restraints should be set upon undeserved payments, as in giving money to street bands or overpaying cabmen. Restraints likewise should be set upon displays of ability in social intercourse : regard should always be had for the feelings of others. In playing a game of skill, for instance, with one whose little boy is a spectator it would be right to play below one's strength and let the father win, lest he should suffer some diminution of admiration on the part of his son. So, too, a man should not generally be defeated in argument or a wit-combat while his *fiancée* is present. Corresponding restraints should be set upon expressions of blame and of praise passed upon others. A lady who after dinner has played badly a piece on the piano should not be thanked, lest she should be encouraged to repeat the infliction on future occasions. A pretty woman who expects glances of admiration should not receive them, lest her vanity be unduly developed. In these small ways Negative Beneficence would increase the allurements of social life. So Spencer says : but some of us may be sceptical, and think that instinct is a better guide than philosophical principles.

"Positive Beneficence."

The injunctions of Positive Beneficence are of a similar character. Marital, parental, and filial beneficence are included in this division of Ethics ; and special emphasis is laid on filial beneficence, or kindness to aged parents, as a duty much neglected at the present time. Aiding the sick and injured, succour to the ill-used and the endangered, pecuniary aid to relatives and friends—all these are named as duties, which, however, are to be intelligently fulfilled, and not carried out promiscuously in a way likely to do more harm than good. Next we reach the question of relief of the poor—commonly but erroneously supposed to occupy almost the whole sphere of beneficence. As already said in dealing with Justice, poor relief is not properly a matter for the State ; and Spencer adduces many arguments to show that compulsory alms-giving and poor laws work injurious effects. It is " a kind of social opium-eating " which leads to ultimate misery far greater than that immediately alleviated. Nevertheless the relief of the poor constitutes a legitimate opportunity for private beneficence. When done with care and personal trouble, it is not only elevating to the character, but may do much good without subsequent harm.

Passing to Social Beneficence, the proposition is put forward that where more imperative claims do not interfere, everyone should enter to some extent into social life, to help and increase the amenities of existence. It is a duty, moreover, to rebel against the various injurious conventions which dominate social life. Such, for instance, is fashion in clothes, which does harm not only by extravagance, but also by demanding an improper amount of time and attention. This expression of opinion on the part of Spencer will perhaps appear to many as a platitude. There are those, however, who hold that, like so many platitudes, it is untrue ; and in a suitable time and place it would not be hard to defend even the vagaries of fashion in women's dress.

Political Beneficence requires men to watch the course of legislation and public business, and to do their share in the promotion of a healthy public life and the prevention of abuses. Incidentally the party system is condemned. If all members of Parliament voted on each question according to their convictions, it would often happen that the Government would find itself in a minority. Under the proposed new conditions, however, that would not involve their resignation. The Government would simply be the servant instead of the master of the House ; and on each question or each law that was proposed the genuine opinion of the representatives of the people would be obtained. Finally it is laid down as a maxim for public life that everything should be presumed to be going wrong until it is proved to be going right. The opportunities and motives for negligence or abuse of power are so numerous, that it is necessary to set up a maxim such as this in order to safeguard the liberties of the people.

At length we reach the end of "The Principles of Ethics," the last volume of the System of Synthetic Philosophy. That the social changes advocated are likely soon to be attained was far from Spencer's expectations. Human nature changes slowly ; and our institutions change only with our natures. But as humanity becomes gradually moulded into more complete harmony with the social State, so will the true principles of Ethics be attained. Those now living can never hope to see the realisation. "While contemplating from the heights of thought, that far-off life of the race never to be enjoyed by them, but only by a remote posterity, they will feel a calm pleasure in the consciousness of having aided the advance towards it."

CHAPTER VIII

METAPHYSICS AND RELIGION [1]

Spencer was not a metaphysician. On the contrary, he refers to metaphysicians with undisguised contempt. Yet it was scarcely possible to attempt a survey of the whole field of knowledge without touching on many of the problems with which metaphysicians endeavour to deal. He professed to be an agnostic both as regards metaphysics and religion ; but in the former sphere he reached conclusions admittedly metaphysical, and in the latter he offered a substitute for religion which came very near to being a shadowy religion itself. Nevertheless his views on these matters stand quite separate from the main body of his works, and it is possible to agree or disagree with them without prejudice to the philosophy as a whole.

" First Principles " is divided into two parts, of which the first, or Metaphysical, portion is entitled " The Unknowable." It might strike the casual observer that if the title correctly indicated the subject, it is curious that Spencer

---

[1] " First Principles," pp. 3—110; " The Nature and Reality of Religion " ; " The Principles of Psychology," vol. ii., pp. 305—520.

should be able to fill more than one hundred pages with a discussion of it. If " The Unknowable " is really unknowable, there is surely nothing more to be said about it ; and the ascription of various attributes to the Unknowable is in reality a sufficient condemnation of the whole doctrine.

The opening sections of the Philosophy set forth the proposition that any widespread human belief, however erroneous it may be in detail, is likely to contain a germ of truth. In all human affairs opinion tends to be widely divergent ; and when the truth is ultimately discovered it is commonly found, Spencer says, that no one of the contending parties was entirely in the right, but that each had succeeded in attaining some portion of the truth. This general doctrine is then applied to the antagonism between science and religion. It is improbable that the disputants on either side are wholly in the right. It is far more probable that each side has seized some part of the truth ; and in order to discover what this may be it is only necessary to elimitate all the antagonistic factors on the two sides and then see what is left. That which is common to both will be the ultimate truth to which science and religion converge.

Dealing in the first place with religion, Spencer says that there are three main types of hypothesis concerning the origin of the universe. It may be self-existent, or self-created, or created by an

external agency. The hypothesis of self-existence
—*i.e.*, that the universe has existed throughout
all eternity — is stated by Spencer to be an
impossible conception. For it involves the idea
of infinite time, which is a thing that cannot be
conceived ; and the theory of self-existence—the
atheistic theory—is not one that can be genuinely
represented in the mind. Yet, as we shall shortly
see, Spencer subsequently referred to the Unknowable as both infinite and eternal.

The theory of self-creation — the pantheistic
theory—is then condemned as equally futile. It
is impossible to imagine the universe arising out
of nothing without a cause : we should be compelled on this hypothesis to suppose that it existed
before in a potential form, which then passed to
the actual form. But this in no way brings an
explanation nearer ; for it is no easier to account
for the origin of a potential universe than of an
actual universe.

The third hypothesis—the theistic view that the
universe was created by an external agency—is
no more tenable than the other two. It only
shifts the problem a step farther back : instead of
inquiring into the origin of the universe, we
have to inquire into the origin of its Creator,
who must either be self-existent or self-created.
But since both these hypotheses have already
been shown to be inconceivable, we are still

no nearer an explanation than we were at the beginning.

Spencer next proceeds to consider what common basis these three divergent hypotheses have. They all agree that there is a mystery to be explained; that there is an inscrutable Power at the back of the universe—something which accounts for the existence of the universe, but which defies all our efforts to understand or even to conceive. It is on this basis alone that a reconciliation can be attained between science and religion.

He then passes from a consideration of the ultimate ideas of religion to a consideration of the ultimate ideas of science. The Kantian doctrine that Space and Time are forms of thought, and therefore subjective, is not one that, in Spencer's opinion, can be truly rendered from words into ideas. We are obliged to regard them as objective; but we are equally unable to conceive Space and Time either as entities or as attributes of entities. They must remain for ever incomprehensible. Matter likewise is beyond our powers of analysis. We cannot conceive it as infinitely divisible; yet we cannot imagine division to be carried so far that no further subdivision can be conceivable. Motion is in the same case. We can only think in terms of relative motion: what absolute motion or absolute rest may be is beyond the powers of human conception. Force and consciousness are likewise inexplicable in their fundamental nature. All these primary concepts of science therefore lead us once more to the recognition of an ultimate mystery, the comprehension of which is beyond the range of any weapon in the armoury of the human intellect.

Spencer then goes on to argue that this fact, to which we are led by induction from the ultimate ideas of science and religion, is strengthened by deduction from the laws of intellectual processes. Knowledge about a thing consists in *classifying* it; that is to say, in associating it with a group of other things already known. Explanations are merely the interpretation of a particular set of events by reference to a more general law. The falling of an apple is " explained " by the law of gravitation; and the progress of knowledge is towards a gradually increasing comprehensiveness of laws : each law is " explained " by inclusion under another law of still wider generality. The widest truth attainable can therefore never be explained : for explanation would take the form of inclusion in some still wider truth; and any ultimate and final truth could only be found at the end of an infinite series ; that is to say, it could never be found at all.

The conclusion thus emerges, continues Spencer, that the ultimate mystery at the bottom of science and religion provides the common factor in which their reconciliation is to be sought. Religion, in bestowing a personal character on this fundamental First Cause, passes beyond the limits of possible knowledge. Science, in assuming that the tools and materials with which it works are the ultimate and unanalysable facts of existence, neglects to take account of that deeper truth on which religion insists. A true religion and a true science both recognise the existence of an ultimate and impenetrable mystery as the First Cause of the universe and of all phenomena. They err only when they proceed to amplify on this First Cause and to endow it with attributes which pass the limit of human knowledge.

Spencer then asks what we are to say about it. It cannot be relative, for if it is the First Cause of everything there is nothing left outside for it to be brought into relation with ; it must therefore be Absolute. We are unable to conceive it as finite : it must therefore be Infinite. We can know nothing of it : we can do no more than refer to it as the Unknowable. Although this doctrine is in opposition to the popular views of religion, it does not follow that the current religion ought to be suddenly extirpated. It is probable that the religion of a people is that which is best suited to their requirements. To a nation that is still incompletely civilised it is good that there should exist a belief in a personal God, who metes out rewards and punishments hereafter. Nevertheless it is incumbent on everyone to speak out as much of the truth as it is given him to perceive.

The first criticism to be made on this attempted reconciliation between science and religion is that, like most compromises, it satisfies neither party. It was hardly to be expected that those who believe in religion would be content with the shadow that is offered them in its place. Religion is far more than the mere contemplation of a mystery. Shorn of all ideas of a God, or of worship, or of personal immortality, little is left but an empty name.

Nor is the proposed reconciliation any more satisfactory to science. "Ultimate mysteries" and "unknowables" are beyond the purview of science, which works only among facts derived by the methods of observation and experiment. Science has something better and more useful to do than contemplate ultimate mysteries. Ignorant people do indeed often reproach science with being unable to "explain the universe," or furnish the answer of some particular question in which they are interested. It would be as reasonable to reproach engineers with their inability to affect the orbit of the moon. It is outside their sphere altogether; and the mystical speculations of common people are no less outside the sphere of science. But just as the engineer may deride a scheme for altering the moon's motion, so may science deride various mystical theories as being totally beyond the capacity of human knowledge. The contemplation of ultimate mysteries is not a part of science, and cannot therefore be made the basis of a reconciliation with religion.

If Spencer's doctrine of the Unknowable had any meaning, it would therefore be false. But in point of fact it is a tissue of meaningless verbiage ; the commonest and most discredited type of Metaphysics. What is meant by Unknowable ? Already, in specifying its existence, knowledge of it is predicated. It is affirmed, firstly, that it exists, and if we know this much of it, it ceases to be altogether unknowable. In the second place, it is affirmed that we neither do nor can know anything of it : which itself is another piece of information about it, derogating still further from the propriety of the title. And then with wonderful inconsistency Spencer proceeds to give us various other items of information about the Unknowable. It is infinite, for instance ; and it is Absolute. Let us examine these two attributes. Why should it be infinite ? Because we cannot imagine it to be finite. But in this shadowy region, why should there not be a third alternative to finite and infinite ? Why not a thousand other alternatives ? Evidently in the region of the Unknowable the same sort of logic and physics hold good as in that of the Knowable. It is not then genuinely unknowable. Its world, after all, becomes more like ours the more we look at it.

Once more we are informed that it is " Absolute "; and here we light upon the most damning absurdity of the whole doctrine. By " absolute " is meant the antithesis of " relative." The stock instance of a " relation " in most books of logic is that of cause and effect. Since the Unknowable is absolute, it does not enter into any relation : it cannot figure either as cause or effect. It lives up in the clouds quite independent of all other existence. And yet Spencer presents it as the final cause of the Knowable. He invents it in order to explain the Knowable. If it is absolute, it cannot explain anything, or be the cause of anything ; its *raison d'être* vanishes entirely. There is in the whole of Spencer's Philosophy no such striking example of looseness of thought as in this theory, which invokes as a cause of the universe a strange monstrosity whose chief attribute is that it cannot enter into a causal or any other relation.[1]

---

[1] Of course, every philosopher must agree that a great many things are and always will be unknowable to the human mind. There is no metaphysics about that. All that is here criticised is " The Unknowable " with a capital U ; a special entity to which Spencer expects you to take off your hat.

Spencer's Metaphysics exhibits to a marked degree all the errors which he so frequently charged against other forms of metaphysics. His entire ignorance of metaphysics, indeed, makes these errors in his case far more conspicuous than in the cases of many of his rivals. It is mere verbiage, carried through by the use of sonorous epithets such as " absolute," " infinite," " unknowable," " impersonal," etc.—all of which mean literally nothing. The whole theory is an attempt to gain popular approval at the outset of his Philosophy by conciliating science and religion. It is a sop to the public—a compromise which last century was so greatly in request, that people would not be likely to examine too closely into its logic. Without wanting to be harsh, we may perhaps observe the Bayswater spirit coming out in this doctrine : there is about it a sort of undisciplined looseness, that cannot stand squarely up to hard facts, and evades issues by the copious use of sesquipedalian terminology.

The Unknowable, which Spencer arrived at in part i. of " First Principles " was subsequently developed by him into a kind of substitute for religion. In the final chapter of " Ecclesiastical Institutions," in the third volume of " The Principles of Sociology," Spencer deals with the " Religious Retrospect and Prospect," wherein he forecasts a time when religion will be reduced purely to the contemplation of the ultimate mystery of the universe. " One truth must grow ever clearer—the truth that there is an Inscrutable Existence everywhere manifested, to which he [man] can neither find nor conceive either beginning or end. Amid the mysteries which become the more mysterious the more they are thought about, there will remain the one absolute certainty, that he is ever in presence of an Infinite and Eternal Energy, from which all things proceed."

This chapter formed the commencement of the controversy with Mr. Frederic Harrison, which was afterwards re-published in the suppressed book " The Nature and Reality of Religion." Mr. Harrison, as a Positivist, defended the religion of humanity as the proper substitute for theology. He ridiculed Spencer's notion that religion could ever be reduced to the contemplation of an empty metaphysical conception, such as the Unknowable. He pointed out that all the emotional and æsthetic elements, which constitute the true basis of religion, were absent from this conception, which also lacked any character of moral exhortation or cultivation of kindly human feeling. And he commented on the theological terminology of the sentence quoted above. For the fulness of religious conviction, Spencer offered for the worship of mankind no more than a cold logical formula,—and he might have added, a formula which breaks down under the first test of logic itself. Nearly all of the very few persons who have had an opportunity of reading this work[1] must agree that Mr. Harrison got very much the better of the controversy ; yet we may suspect that the religion of the future may be wholly different from what either of these two philosophers imagined. It is doubtless more likely to assume an emotional form than to be a mere intellectual formula, which never has yet, and never will, sway the deeper convictions of mankind. But we are not at present called upon to offer any alternative forecast. It is quite clear that the doctrine of the Unknowable is untenable in philosophy ; Mr. Harrison has shown that it is useless for religion. It is more interesting to note the air of reverence with which Spencer regarded the Unknowable as he grew older. Spencer professed himself to be an agnostic ; but his agnosticism travelled in the course of years from the verge of Atheism to the verge of Theology. As a young man he would no doubt have resented the charge of Atheism, just as much as, when an old man, he would have resented the charge of Theology. Yet he differed from Atheism scarcely more than in name ; and his *rapprochement* to Theology (which he would probably have denied)

[1] Kindly lent to me by Mr. Geoffrey Williams, of Messrs. Williams and Norgate.

is not wholly free from the suspicion of playing to the gallery ; or rather, let it be said, of allowing his thoughts to be swayed by the force of popular belief. It is certainly rarer for an old man to hold out against the infection of popular senti- ment than for a young man ; and to one reading his essays and correspondence at this period there is an indefinable sense of drifting with the stream, and of an exceptional willingness to meet popular feeling half-way. The influence of Youmans was then strong; and Spencer was undoubtedly animated by a desire to obtain at least the approval of his American admirers.

In only one other section of the Philosophy do we come again on metaphysical doctrines—namely, in the " General Analysis," constituting part vii. in the second volume of " The Principles of Psychology." We are here introduced to a new theory of knowledge and a criticism of the doctrine of Idealism.

After various preliminaries Spencer reaches the important question as to what we are to adopt as a criterion of truth ? In judging between realism and idealism, by what test are we to decide the relative accuracy of the mental processes by which these opposite deliverances are attained ?

The propositions which go to constitute an argument or a statement have first to be reduced to their simplest form ; and the final test of their truth in each case is stated by Spencer to be the inconceivability of their negation. On touching a body in the dark, for instance, we immediately have a sensation of resistance, with which arises also the idea of extension. If, now, we wish to determine the truth of the general proposition "whatever resists has extension," our mode of procedure is to endeavour to conceive resistance without extension. Since no mental effort enables us to form such a conception, we are justified in saying that the proposition " whatever resists has extension " is a truth of the highest certainty that can be attained by human intelligence.

The ultimate test of the truth of any proposition, then, is found in our inability to conceive its negation ; and this test is called by Spencer the Universal Postulate. An argument or chain of reasoning consists of a succession of steps, at each of which the Universal Postulate is applied— since we pass from one step to another by noting that the second is inevitably involved in the first— by an inability to conceive the second not following the first. When we have two chains of reasoning leading to different conclusions, we must give the preference to that which has the fewest links—*i.e.*, invokes the Universal Postulate the least frequently. We must give it the preference, not because there is any weakness in the Postulate itself, but because it is always liable to be wrongly

applied : we may imagine that we cannot conceive
the negation of a proposition, when in reality we
can conceive it. Hence, the fewer steps there are in
a chain of reasoning, the smaller will be the chance
of error in the conclusion ; and Realism is greatly
superior to Idealism, in that it requires only one
application of the Universal Postulate, while
Idealism requires several. The realistic hypothesis
presents itself as an elementary proposition of
which the negation is inconceivable, whereas the
idealistic hypothesis is alleged by Spencer to be
reached by a succession of such elementary propositions. The room for error in the establishment
of Idealism is therefore as many times greater
than in the establishment of Realism as there
are steps required for the argument. By a further
analysis it is shown that the realistic belief is a
necessary deliverance of consciousness. All our
thoughts are determined by the relative cohesion
among our component states of consciousness ;
and where two trains of thought differ the only
way of deciding between them is to compare
the strength of cohesion of the ideas in the two
cases.

Whereas Idealism is thus wholly discredited,
the Realism which is forced upon us is not the
crude Realism of the peasant, but a " Transfigured
Realism." We are prohibited from believing
that external objects are in their absolute nature

just as they appear to us to be. For they are known to us only through our senses : the *object* is known relatively only to the *subject*. We must therefore regard the object as an appearance : objective existence as it appears to us is phenomenal, not noumenal. There is behind it the Unknowable Reality of which we can predicate and imagine nothing (but of which Spencer elsewhere both predicated and imagined much). Objective existence is a mode of the Unknowable ; and subjective existence is another mode. The Realism we have arrived at is not an absolute Realism, but a relative Realism. For we can predicate *absolute* reality only of the Unknowable. The hypothesis of Idealism has therefore served its purpose in discrediting Crude Realism. The true realism is that called Transfigured Realism, which is based upon the most certain of all deliverances of consciousness.

This sums up the whole of Spencer's Metaphysics. The candid reader will perhaps not perceive any wide difference in the nature of the arguments used from those commonly employed in the Metaphysics which he condemns. The whole argument itself constitutes a long deductive chain, at each link of which there is on Spencer's own principle a fresh liability to error. This particular mode of establishing Transfigured Realism seems to involve many more links in the chain of argument than that by which Idealism is established. It is perhaps hardly worth while to criticise in further detail a doctrine which is probably not now held by a single competent philosopher of any school whatever.

CHAPTER IX

EVOLUTION

THE metaphysical portion of Spencer's Philosophy is a comparatively unimportant part of the whole. It is also quite separate from and irrelevant to the rest; and we may therefore pursue our studies of his writings without any bias derived from our opinion of his Metaphysics. The largest single doctrine of the Philosophy is that of universal Evolution, formally set forth in "First Principles." The main purpose of the Philosophy, indeed, is to establish a general law of Evolution which holds good in every department of knowledge; and Spencer contends that the true sphere of Philosophy is not in the province of metaphysics, but in dealing with those universal laws which transcend the limits of any individual science. For the convenience of scientific workers, knowledge is broken up into a number of separate compartments, each of which becomes the preoccupation of a special class of men of science. But these divisions have no real objective existence. They are what Lamarck would have called "*parties de l'art.*" Spencer conceived the function of philosophy to be that of formulating laws which transcend the limits of any individual science. He reached this conception by a mode of argument similar to that used in his reconciliation of science and religion— namely, by finding the greatest common measure of agreement in all conflicting opinions as to the true subject-matter of Philosophy. As a result of this method he concluded that Philosophy deals with knowledge of the highest generality. In each of the separate sciences generalisations are attained which apply to all the classes of objects with which those sciences respectively deal. There are certain general truths of biology, of physics, of astronomy, etc. In biology, for instance, we may draw the generalisation that the temperature of animals is proportional to the amount of molecular change occurring within them. But these truths are confined in their application to the objects with which the science in question deals. There are truths of a still higher order of generality, and which are not bounded by the limits of the special sciences. It is to the study of these that the name of philosophy must be applied. Philosophy is completely unified knowledge, in opposition to the partially unified knowledge of science.

Spencer begins his exposition by affirming that the difference between mind and matter, or between subject and object, is the widest and most fundamental difference that the human intellect can grasp. He then proceeds to vindicate the doctrine of the Indestructibility of Matter. He characteristically defends this doctrine, not only on inductive grounds, but on account of the impossibility of conceiving a portion of matter in empty space, which should disappear without leaving any trace whatever. Since matter is only known to us through the force which it exerts upon us, the indestructibility of matter implies the indestructibility of the force exerted by matter. The continuity of motion is dealt with on similar lines. If motion were liable to appear and to vanish at random, none of the conclusions of science could have been reached, nor could the activities of normal life be carried on. The continuity of motion implies and corresponds to what is more generally known as Conservation of Energy.

These two laws—the indestructibility of matter and the continuity of motion — are special cases of one law still more general, named by Spencer the Persistence of Force. For there are, he says, two different kinds of force — that by which matter becomes known as existing and that by which it becomes known as acting. As already mentioned, matter can only be known by the force which it exerts upon us ; and thus, in plain terms, the two kinds of existing forces are matter and energy. Both of these are unalterable in quantity, and liable only to transformations from one kind of matter or energy into another kind of matter or energy. Hence it follows that force—the ultimate form of all existence—is likewise unalterable in quantity : it persists. Nevertheless this great truth is one that transcends demonstration ; for its assumption is involved in every experiment or observation undertaken to prove it. It is the widest of all truths, and is therefore not capable of being comprehended under any other.

If force is persistent, it follows that the relations between forces are also persistent ; and this is simply another way of expressing the Uniformity of Law. Where a certain set of conditions is realised, from which a particular result has been found to flow, then wherever precisely the same conditions are realised on another occasion, precisely the same result as before will ensue. For otherwise we must suppose that some new force has come into existence out of nothing, or that some old force has fallen utterly out of existence ; and any such opinion is contrary to the law of the Persistence of Force. The uniformity of law, the invariable sequence of the same consequents upon the same antecedents, lies of course at the base of the whole experimental method.

The next step in the argument is an account of the transformation and equivalence of forces : a physical truth too well known to need much comment. Everyone is aware that motion, though its energy cannot be destroyed, is transformable into heat, sound, light, etc. Any one form of energy is, at least theoretically, capable of being changed into any other form of energy. The planetary motions of the Solar System are adequately accounted for by the forces generated as the different portions of the system fell together from the remote distances which originally separated them. Geologic changes arise from the yet unexpended heat of nebular condensation. Plant-life abounds most luxuriously in those regions of the earth where the sun radiates the greatest amount of light and heat; and the distribution of animal life closely follows that of plant-life.

Through the first five editions of " First Principles " this part of the argument ended here ; but with the sixth or final edition a new addition was made which appears to have been in every way unfortunate, for Spencer went so far as to affirm that physical forces might be transformed into mental forces. That is to say, that when some physical force, such as light or heat, affected the organism, that force might be absolutely converted into a state of consciousness, which again could be re-converted into some other physical force. He admitted, indeed, that the transformation was not easy to observe quantitatively. A minute stimulus, such as that involved in tickling, may produce a great volume of feeling as compared with which a more powerful stimulus would have produced a far smaller volume. So, too, the infinitesimal stimulus of a word or a sight may produce boundless emotions, while yet other very similar words and sights may produce scarcely any emotion at all. But Spencer stoutly affirmed that there did exist some proportion between the force used and the consciousness resulting ; and he was led in consequence to attack Huxley's Automaton Theory, which denied to consciousness any motive power whatever. Concerning this belief of Spencer's, that physical force might be converted into feelings or ideas or other states of consciousness, it has only to be said that the theory runs counter to the whole doctrine of the physical conservation of energy, and moreover that no evidence of any kind is tendered in support of it. It seems, indeed, to conflict with Spencer's own frequently repeated statement that the gulf between mind and matter cannot be bridged, but that these two classes of experience are completely and entirely separate.

He then goes on to illustrate the transformation of forces in social life : stating that the amount of activity produced by any society is proportional to the quantities of physical force with which it is supplied by its environment. This proposition is illustrated by the fact that a good harvest leads to vigorous activity in every sphere of business ; and the social forces thus set in motion are derived through the yield of wheat from the energy of solar radiation. This proposition again seems susceptible to criticism ; for it is difficult to see in what respect a good harvest may be described as a force. It is not a question solely of the amount of light and heat received from the sun, for beyond a certain limit these do much more harm than good. Moreover, it is not found by experience that races living in those countries where the supply of physical force is most prodigal are any more vigorous or active than those living in less favoured climates.

Spencer next deals with the direction and rhythm of motion. A body moves either in the direction of greatest traction or in that of least resistance. The planets move round the sun in orbits which are controlled by the central force of gravitation, modified by the minor forces which give rise to perturbations. The denudation of the earth's surface is effected by the force which draws water towards the centre of the earth. In the organic world, natural selection indicates the path of least resistance. In physiological and mental processes, as well as in social life, the actions which take place are the resultant of all the forces at work. Motion similarly is not regular, but rhythmical.

The periodic character of planetary motions provides an instance ; and the truth holds good throughout all orders of existences down to the pulsations of dancing and poetry, and the varying rise and fall of birth-rates, crime, disease, etc. Undulation is a general rule to which all events in the universe conform.

Spencer had now formulated a series of philosophic laws which he regarded as holding good of all classes of objects in the universe. He next turned to the discovery of a formula under which the consequences of these laws might be expressed. The universe appeared to him to consist wholly of matter and motion or force ; for, as already seen, he considered that consciousness might be converted into motion, just as motion might be converted into heat. But the matter and motion existing throughout the universe was not stationary ; it was continually undergoing change, and the formula which he sought was one which summed up in a single law the characteristics of this change in every department.

The first and most important characteristic was that matter constantly tended to become " integrated " ; that is to say, to be pressed together more compactly. Motion, on the other hand, tended to become dissipated or degraded ; and, instead of being highly concentrated at certain points, to be scattered more uniformly throughout the universe. An obvious illustration came to hand in the nebular theory of the solar system. We must suppose that the matter of which that system is now composed was originally spread over a vastly larger area than it occupies at present. Each planet, from having been gaseous, has contracted into a compact ball. Here we have an illustration of the integration of matter. At the same time, the motion contained in the original nebula has been dissipated as heat in the course of integration. Other characteristics of evolution are found in increasing heterogeneity, coherence, and definiteness. The original nebula was comparatively homogeneous throughout. It has now broken up into a number of discrete and heterogeneous bodies. There was originally little coherence between its parts. The parts of the evolved planets, however, are closely coherent, and the entire system is bound by gravitation into a united whole. And again the boundaries of the nebula were vague and indefinite: the boundaries of the bodies which have arisen from it are sharply marked off and definite.

On this latter argument Professor William James has made the criticism that the outlines of a nebula are in reality no less definite than those of a solid body. The indefiniteness is apparent only, due to the greater difficulty of indicating the exact outer boundary of the nebula. But the points at which the most outlying material particles of the nebula exist are just as definite in real fact and in position as the points which constitute the surface of a planet. The criticism appears to be founded in part on imperfect apprehension of the theory criticised.

Spencer next went on to trace a parallel series of transformations on the earth. The integration of matter by contraction is still in progress. Heterogeneity has immensely increased between its various parts. Coherence and definiteness, as well as heterogeneity, are shown by the sharp separation of land and sea; the gradual assumption of a permanent geographical form, with fixed mountains, valleys, rivers, etc. In life the same tendency is observed. The primitive protozoa, such as *Amœba*, have little coherence between their parts: their structure is indefinite and changeable; and their substance is comparatively homogeneous throughout. In man, at the opposite end of the animal scale, the parts are closely coherent: the structure is definite and fixed within very narrow variations; the body itself has attained a high degree of heterogeneity. A striking integration has also taken place; for each organ or part is entirely dependent upon the co-operation of all the other organs and parts. The animal is integrated into a single unit or individuality.

The human mind as well as language and the

products of society pass through a corresponding series of changes. It is characteristic of advanced thought to be *definite* and *coherent*. In highly developed languages each word has a sharply defined signification. Great heterogeneity has arisen among the different kinds of words, which also have become integrated into short syllables from their original long and cumbrous form. Human implements betray the same concatenation of changes. The early flint implement was indefinite in shape and incoherent in structure. It has developed into the vast heterogeneity of implements now used in civilised society; and the most developed of these are absolutely definite in shape and integrated into a coherent unity, in the sense that one part of them would be useless without the whole. The same law applies to music, dancing, poetry, etc., and all manifestations of the human mind.

In biology, once again, organisms have become integrated into compact groups. An immense heterogeneity has arisen among them out of their primitive homogeneity. They are sharply defined from one another, etc. The differentiation and integration characterising social progress is of the same order. From primitive societies, in which there was much homogeneity among the occupations and conditions of all its members, there has arisen a state of society with innumerable

sharply defined grades both of rank and occupation. Division of labour has taken the place
of the original homogeneity. Integration and
coherence are illustrated by the interdependence
of the different sections of society. No one portion
could be cut off and live by itself independently
of the remainder, as can happen in an unorganised
society. Among every order of existences, then,
from the largest to the smallest, from the most
concrete to the most abstract, evolution is characterised by the same series of transformations ; and
the law of evolution is to be formulated as follows :
*Evolution is an integration of matter and concomi-
tant dissipation of motion ; during which the matter
passes from a relatively indefinite, incoherent homogeneity to a relatively definite, coherent heterogeneity,
and during which the retained motion undergoes a
parallel transformation.*

When Spencer had attained this formula by
inductive methods he at once endeavoured to
place it on a deductive basis by proving its necessary derivation from the law of the Persistence of
Force—his primary *datum* of consciousness. In
doing so he said that we should attain a complete
unification of knowledge—the deduction from a
single primary law of all the different kinds of
events occurring throughout the universe. This
unification is achieved by naming four general
principles which flow necessarily from the doc-

trine of the Persistence of Force. They are the Instability of the Homogeneous, the Multiplication of Effects, Segregation, and Equilibration.

No homogeneous body, Spencer argued, can preserve its original homogeneity when exposed to the action of external forces. For any incident force must affect its different parts in different ways; the exterior will be differently affected from the interior, etc. There is an inevitable tendency to increasing heterogeneity. This tendency is further accentuated by the multiplication of effects. An external force acting upon a body must become broken up into a number of different forces, in consequence of the different reactions of the various parts of the body. A single cause will have innumerable different effects reverberating throughout the entire system. Hence heterogeneity is set up: the homogeneous condition is unstable. Further, when once heterogeneity has set in, external incident forces will act similarly on similar parts of the body, and differently on different parts. Similar parts will thus be forced into the same channel: segregation will be established, so that the like parts of the body will be collected together in one place, and the unlike parts will be separated out. We thus obtain an explanation of the *definiteness* characteristic of advancing evolution. Instances are furnished by the pebbles on a beach, which tend to be segregated together in accordance with their size : by differentiation of function in organisms, whereby the general substance of the animal and plant lose their power of carrying out all the functions needed by the organism, and each function receives a special organ and localised situation : by division of labour in society, etc., etc.

Evolution, however, according to Spencer, is not an infinite process : after continuing for a certain period, it leads to equilibrium ; either the absolute equilibrium of death, or the moving equilibrium displayed by the present state of the solar system, or in the life of a single animal or plant. Moreover, Dissolution—the reverse process of Evolution—is liable to occur. In dissolution, the transformations undergone are precisely opposed to those of evolution. A reversal of the stellar system to the nebular condition is an instance of dissolution ; so also is the death of an organism, accompanied by dissipation of its substance, by loss of definiteness and coherence in its structure, and by the resumption of a comparatively homogeneous form. The decay of a nation is a further instance of dissolution : the emigration and scattering of its members constitutes the dissipation of matter ; the breakdown of division of labour is a reversion to homogeneity. The universe, therefore, is in a perpetual state of flux. It passes from evolution through equilibrium to dissolution, and from dissolution again to evolution. And all this, while inductively ascertained, is regarded by Spencer as a necessary deduction from the law of the Persistence of Force—the ultimate fact of consciousness, and the highest expression of unified knowledge.

We here reach the end of " First Principles." It is not easy to form an estimate of the truth of Spencer's general law of Evolution. Certain parts of the argument appear to be ill-founded, notably the attempt to deduce it from the Persistence of Force. It is highly ingenious ; but is somewhat reminiscent of Spencer's engineering inventions, which were not successful in practice. From the point of view of a man of science, the method of deduction is greatly overdone, and excites no confidence whatever. The many dangers and traps attending that method are such as to render it of very little value in such a sphere as that in which Spencer used it. It is plain enough to the biographer how Spencer reached the theory. From a casual remark of von Baer, he gradually perceived that animal development proceeds towards the heterogeneous, coherent, and definite. Being interested in astronomy, he quickly apprehended the fact that the change of a nebula into stars implied a similar concatenation of changes. A generalisation was at once formed ; and all the rest of the universe was forced into

the mould without further ado, whether it really
fitted or not.   And it must be admitted that it
does seem as a rule to fit more or less accurately.
The future must decide whether Spencer has
presented a true and genuinely significant account
of evolution in the universe.   Up to now it can
only be said that the discovery, if genuine, has
proved sterile.   It has led to no progress in any
branch of science : it is, indeed, too uncertain a
hypothesis to argue from.   Yet it is undeniably
interesting, and may represent not only a truth,
but a profound one.   It is not discredited by
Spencer's failure to prove it, nor by the lightness
of some of his arguments.   It was his character to
produce his doctrine in a form of finality, well-
rounded and established for ever on the most
secure basis.   But it is not in the nature of
things that such a theory should be indubitably
established by all the laws of physics and logic
the moment it was discovered.   If he had put it
forward merely as a suggestion, the critics would
have been much quieter ; but when a pistol is held
at our heads, and we are called upon to accept it
as being in much the same category as the law of
gravitation, then we are bound to protest.

CHAPTER X

BIOLOGY

After formulating the law of Universal Evolution, it was Spencer's original intention to write a succession of works, in which the operation of that law should be traced in the various departments of concrete science. The first of these works was to deal with " The Principles of Astrogeny," or the evolution of nebulæ into the stars and solar system. The second was to be " The Principles of Geogeny," giving an account of the development of the earth. And then there were to follow the works on Biology, Psychology, Sociology, and Ethics, in their natural order of increasing specialisation. These four latter works were indeed actually written, and, in conjunction with " First Principles," now constitute the Synthetic Philosophy. But the volumes dealing with Astrogeny and Geogeny were never begun. The execution of the entire work was too large a task for a single man. Moreover, Spencer was less interested in these two more elementary departments ; and the working of the law of Evolution was in their case more obvious and less in need of exposition than in the more complex regions of Biology, Psychology, and their subordinate sciences. Nevertheless, he did not wholly neglect the subject of Inorganic Evolution ; and these two gaps in his Philosophy are filled in rough outline by the two essays in "Essays," vol. i., entitled "The Nebular Hypothesis" and "Illogical Geology."

Spencer begins his "Principles of Biology" by a discussion of the chemical composition of living organisms. They are, he says, constituted almost entirely out of four elements in various combination—oxygen, hydrogen, nitrogen, and carbon. The first three of these are gases, which for long defied any attempt to liquefy them ; the last is a solid, and remains solid except at extremely high temperatures. Nitrogen and carbon, moreover, are among the most inert substances known. From considerations of this character Spencer argues that the substance of which organic matter is made is of exceedingly mobile constitution, and enters with great readiness into new forms of combination. As a result of this circumstance, organic matter responds with exceptional facility to the operation of external forces. Heat, light, and chemical agencies, acting upon it, easily produce changes of molecular arrangement, yet without causing decomposition. In short, Spencer regarded organic matter as so constituted as to be singularly plastic or modifiable by external action. It is chemically affected by the environment far more readily than inorganic matter. It is admirably designed for undergoing constant change without degradation.

Proceeding next to a definition of Life, Spencer insists that change is the most characteristic feature of living matter. An organism is the seat of constant change, owing to the processes of assimilation, reproduction, metabolism, etc. Yet these changes are not haphazard : they occur in direct response to forces of the environment. Thus a man may perceive some danger while it is yet far off and take measures for its avoidance. That is to say, there occurs in the man a change of activity, in correspondence to a certain external event—namely, a threatening external danger. A worm, on the other hand, might remain quite unconscious of the danger, and take no precautions for its avoidance ; that is to say, no internal change would occur in the worm as a consequence of the external event. There is less complete correspondence between the worm and its environment ; and the life of the worm is by that amount less than the life of the man. Spencer in fact regards the universe as the scene of constant change. An organism is a small portion of chemically complex matter, likewise exhibiting incessant change. Life consists in the correspondence between the changes of the organism with the changes occurring in its environment. When for every change in the environment a corresponding change takes place in the organism, the quantity of life is high. But when occurrences in the environment evoke no response in the organism the quantity of life is low.

In the " General Synthesis " of vol. i. of " The Principles of Psychology " Spencer further elaborates this doctrine. He points out that the correspondence or reaction of the organism is at first limited to few and homogeneous occurrences in the environment, but that in the higher forms of life it becomes more heterogeneous : organisms can react to more radical changes in the environment ; the tentacles of a zoophyte, for instance, contract on being touched. With increasing intensity of life the correspondence becomes extended both in space and time. Dealing first with space, it is clear that the most primitive organisms react to the environment only through actual contact. An amœba betrays no consciousness of the neighbourhood of food until touched by it. With the development of the special senses, however, organisms begin to react to objects that are yet at a distance. They make movements to approach food, or to escape an enemy. In this way the correspondence between inner and outer events is extended in space, until among human beings we arrive at the Astronomer, whose inner relations accurately correspond to outer relations fixed at an incredible distance away. The correspondence is likewise developed in time, from the lowest animals which only know the passing moment to human beings who make their arrangements to correspond with long sequences of outer events, and who look forward far into the future and backward far into the past.

The correspondence likewise increases in speciality. It is at first rude and inaccurate, it becomes specialised and precise. A low organism can make very few distinctions among surrounding objects. A higher organism has a much more refined perception. It can distinguish particles of food-material from particles of a deleterious or indifferent character, and can regulate its activities accordingly. Among human beings, surrounding forces can be distinguished down to very minute shades, and can be met by adaptations equally detailed and specialised. The process is carried further by the manufacture of scientific instruments, by means of which distances or lengths (for example) can be measured with a very high degree of accuracy, thus establishing an extremely precise correspondence between inner and outer relations.

Although the evolution of life is characterised by an increasing speciality of the correspondences, it is likewise characterised by an increasing generality of correspondences. This truth is illustrated by the power of perceiving *attributes* as apart from *things*. A human being, after perceiving a number of red objects, can form the abstract idea of redness. The correspondence with the environment thus increases in generality until it culminates in the wide generalisations of science, whereby inner relations are brought into harmony with excessively generalised outer relations. The correspondences once again increase in complexity : a higher organism can deal with far more complex external situations than a lower organism can. Integration of the correspondences is shown by the fact that the reactions of an animal become after practice nearly automatic. Many complicated movements become welded into one. Incidentally it is pointed out that intelligence is proportional to the tactual powers of the organism. The greater its capacity for manipulation of an external object, the higher its understanding. As a result of all this discussion Spencer formulates the following definition of Life. It is : *The definite combination of heterogeneous changes, both simultaneous and successive, in correspondence with external coexistences and sequences.* For practical purposes, he says, this is the most serviceable definition of life; but it may be expressed in a still more abstract form as : *The continuous adjustment of internal relations to external relations.*

Although furnishing a definition of Life, this

formula in no way explains the dynamic element in life ; nor does it enlighten us as to what life really is. On this subject, there is the hypothesis of a vital principle, accounting for the special activities of animals and plants. The hypothesis however, is altogether untenable and must be rejected. Yet we are still wholly unable to see how physico-chemical forces can give rise to the innumerable and varied manifestations of life, and especially to actions which are said to have a purpose. Spencer winds up this discussion by the remark that we are here confronted with one of the ultimate mysteries to which science leads us on every side. " Life as a principle of activity is unknown and unknowable."

" The Inductions of Biology," which are next dealt with, contain a number of the generally recognised principles of that science, with a few original theories, of which the more important only can here be named. Growth is an integration of matter—the absorption into the organism of environing substances. The amount of growth depends upon the surplus of nutrition over expenditure, but is determined also by the initial size of the animal or plant at the commencement of growth. Development is from lower to higher complexity—from relative homogeneity to relative heterogeneity. At first the lowly organism is almost without structure, but gradually differentiation takes place: the special organs make their appearance; and with increasing complexity of structure goes increasing complexity of function. In primitive organisms every part of the body carries on all the necessary functions : assimilation, reproduction, locomotion, etc.   In developed organisms there is established a " physiological division of labour " : the general protoplasm has lost its universal powers; and each different function is carried out by a special organ suited for it.   As regards both structure and function, homogeneity gives way to heterogeneity; and integration is shown by the increasing interdependence of the separate organs and their functions in place of the comparative self-sufficiency of the different parts of the primitive organism.

After naming the chief facts of adaptation— the close correspondence between an organism and its environment—and after discussing what constitutes an individual, we are brought to the subject of heredity.   It is first pointed out that offspring resemble their parents, not only in general features, but in small details.   The inheritance of acquired characters is insisted upon.   That is to say, when an animal (or plant) has undergone some modification of structure on account of use or disuse of the part, that modification is liable, by Spencer's theory, to be inherited like any other variation.   We may expect the son of a blacksmith to be born with potentially stronger arms than other children. So, too, when any structure is disused from generation to generation, and when in consequence it is poorly developed in each generation, that feeble development will become fixed in the hereditary constitution, and in course of time with continued disuse the structure will altogether disappear.

It is unnecessary to comment further on the much-discussed hypothesis that acquired characters are hereditary. Suffice it to say that no evidence has yet been produced in proof of that belief, which is now entertained only by a negligible minority of biologists. As already stated, however, it was at one time regarded by Spencer as the one and only factor in organic evolution; for no better reason than that before the discovery of natural selection he could think of no other factor.

How is the fact of heredity to be accounted for ? How is it that the microscopic human ovum proceeds to develop until it assumes an appearance closely resembling that of its progenitors ? Spencer adopts the analogy of a crystal; for an inorganic substance always crystallises into the same form. In this case the fact is due to molecular polarity; that is to say, the molecules fall into an arrangement in which their axes all point in one direction. A similar explanation must be sought in the case of organisms. They must be composed of certain units which tend to arrange themselves into the structure characteristic of the species. These units, however, cannot be chemical; for the molecules of organic matter do not show the great variety that the theory requires. Nor can they be morphological; for heredity is obviously not due to any special arrangement of cells. They must therefore be intermediate between these two : they must consist of particular groups of molecules, and may be termed " physiological units " or, better still, " constitutional units." The special structure of an animal or plant must be due to the special constitutional units of the organisms, which (as in crystals) tend to fall into the specific arrangement characteristic of the species to which they belong. The theory differs from Darwin's theory of gemmules in that it regards the constitutional units as being all alike, whereas gemmules are of as many different kinds as there are tissues or organs in the body. It differs also from Weismann's theory, partly because Weismann's units, like Darwin's, are of many different kinds, and partly because it does not recognise the division between germ-plasm and soma-plasm, to which Weismann attached so much importance.

The reasons are next considered for the mingling of the substance of two separate organisms in sexual reproduction. The constitutional units of any individual tend to equilibration ; that is to

say, they become fixed and react less readily to
the operation of incident forces. By fusion with
the constitutional units of another similar individual an element of instability is introduced.
The new constitutional units are restored to their
needful plasticity; they are readily affected by
incident forces, and they can respond to those
forces by a renewed activity of growth and development. Were it not for this fusion, the specific
form would quickly become set hard and lose
its plasticity; there would no longer be adequate correspondence between the changes in the
organism and those in the environment, and life
would come to an end.

After drawing up a classification of animals and
plants, Spencer passes to the subject of Distribution. The argument here is that, whether we
consider the distribution of organisms in space or
in time, we find no evidence of any intelligent
disposition, but only of a blind evolution which
has by slow degrees brought about the state of
affairs now existing. With this argument " The
Inductions of Biology " come to an end.

The next division of " The Principles of Biology "
is devoted to the Evolution of Life. The hypothesis that each species was separately created is
first considered. It fails to account for the great
majority of the acknowledged facts: the existence
for instance of evil in the world appears to imply

a Creator who is either deficient in morality or else deficient in power. Moreover, the actual creation of a species is a proposition which cannot be translated from words into ideas. It is definitely unthinkable, and therefore presents, not a genuine explanation, but a pseudo-explanation.

We are therefore thrown back upon the theory of evolution, against which none of the foregoing objections can be raised. The theory has the further credentials that it was first originated among the most highly instructed men of an intellectual era, instead of being derived, like the hypothesis of special creation, from the superstitions of barbaric times. It is moreover supported by four converging lines of evidence. The first of these is derived from the facts of classification. Animals and plants fall naturally into groups and sub-groups. A collection of species, not very different from one another, are comprised within a genus : genera again fall naturally into orders and classes. In short, the resemblances between species of animals and plants are just such as to suggest relationship, just such as they would be if they were all descended from a common ancestor : these resemblances, on the other hand, are quite unaccountable by the hypothesis of special creation.

In the second place, the study of embryology shows that each individual animal and plant

does in fact pass through the same series of transformations as is alleged of the whole species.
Every individual begins life as a single comparatively homogeneous cell. All individuals thus
start their development from the same point,
and become gradually differentiated to the widely
divergent types proper to their species. This
fact forcibly suggests that the species themselves
come from one stock.

In the third place, the shapes of the adult
organisms show a fundamental kinship, not otherwise accountable. The existence of rudimentary
organs, which have no function, cannot be explained except on the assumption that they are
survivals from a time when they possessed
genuine utility. The rudiments of teeth in birds
and of legs in snakes are difficult to reconcile with
special creation, but at once receive an explanation if birds are derived from animals which had
teeth and snakes from animals which had legs.

The fourth line of argument is supplied by the
distribution of organisms in space and time. A
study of fossils shows that those found in recent
strata are more akin to living forms than those
found in deeper strata. As regards geographical
distribution, the facts observed do not bear out
the hypothesis that each species was specially
created in adaptation to its environment; but
they do bear out the hypothesis that they have

been modified by evolution to harmony with their
surroundings.

Given that Evolution is a true theory, it remains
to record the mode by which it came about. It
is needless to describe Spencer's presentation of
evolution, which was closely similar to that of
Darwin and his other contemporaries. He named
two factors—the inheritance of acquired characters
and natural selection. He expressed the view that
in early stages of evolution natural selection was
the main factor, but that in course of time it was
gradually superseded by inheritance of acquired
characters, until in the case of man natural
selection was scarcely operative at all. This part
of " The Principles of Biology " derives some
historical interest from the fact that Spencer here
coined and used for the first time the phrase
" Survival of the Fittest " as a synonym for
Natural Selection.

The second volume of " The Principles of
Biology " opens with a section on " Morphological
Development," where one or two questions of
interest are discussed. Spencer regarded all the
parts of a plant—the stem, branches, leaves,
flowers, etc.—as representing divergent lines of
evolution from one type of primitive frond, such
as we find in seaweed. A phanerogamic plant
consists, according to him, of a cluster or group
of such fronds, which have become specialised

in different directions to form the parts of the plant.

He held that animals were in the same way compounds of many elementary and homogeneous units. Thus an annulate creature like a centipede or earthworm is in reality a chain of similar individuals, incompletely separated from one another. With the progress of evolution a higher degree of integration is attained, until among insects the successive rings are less conspicuous ; and the appearance is more that of a single complete animal than of a chain of simpler animals fused together. In spiders and crabs the integration is still more complete. But Spencer wisely precludes this theory from explaining the segmentation of the vertebrate skeleton.

From the subject of morphological integration, Spencer next turns to that of differentiation. What are the factors which cause the specific shapes of animals and plants ? What is it that controls the polarisation of the constitutional units and causes the various tissues to grow out into the particular shapes characteristic of them ? The fundamental principle which provides the answer to this question is that " in any organism equal amounts of growth take place in those directions in which the incident forces are equal." Take for instance the leaf of a tree. Its upper and under surfaces are very differently situated as regards the environment. The upper surface is far more exposed to many incident forces—the light and warmth of the sun, etc. —than the lower surface. In consequence there is a great difference of form between the upper and lower surfaces. The two sides of the leaf, on the other hand, are not exposed to any difference between the incident forces which on the average affect them. Wind, rain, light, etc., fall upon them as frequently on one side as upon the other. Hence the two sides are alike, and the leaf itself is bilaterally symmetrical.

In the sea-anemone, again, the environment acts very differently upon the lower part attached to the ground from what it does on the free upper part. Hence a striking difference between the structures above and below. Food, however, is equally liable to approach it from any side. The forces of the environment do not act upon it differently upon one side from any other side. Hence the animal presents to its environment the same structure on every side. It exhibits a radial symmetry; and this constant form has been impressed upon it, in the course of a long evolution, by those external forces which have in the long run acted upon it equally from every side. In the *Annulosa* again—in centipedes and insects—the diverse character of the forces acting upon the anterior and the posterior segments have caused marked differentiation between the anterior and posterior extremities. In mammals the same truth is exhibited to a still higher degree. In mammals, again, the forces acting upon one side of the organism are in no way different, in the long run, from those acting upon the other side : hence mammals are bilaterally symmetrical. At the other end of the scale, creatures like amœba, which are affected equally by the environment on every side, are altogether amorphous. Such differentiation of structure as they exhibit is that of exterior and interior, etc., where indeed the incident forces are different.

The remainder of this division of the " Biology " is devoted to an account of the origin of the vertebrate skeleton. As already observed, vertebrates cannot be regarded, like annulose animals, as compounded of a series of individuals incompletely separated off from one another. Why, then, have they a segmented skeleton ? Taking a fish as an example, the lateral flexions and extensions of its body in swimming must establish certain mechanical stresses and strains in its body-substance. The part of its body least affected by these forces is its central axis. This, therefore, may and must become differentiated from the more lateral portions. Being less bent from side to side, it becomes less pliant, more rigid, and finally develops into bone. The need for some bending from side to side produces, however, a series of lateral incisions, which, while leaving the main axis of sufficient strength to serve for muscular support, yet ensures the requisite flexibility. Ordinary mechanical principles in fact are quite sufficient to account for the origin of this series of lateral incisions. The intervening portions of the column become the vertebræ. Where there is no need for flexibility, as in the skull, there is no segmentation; and the theory of Goethe and Oken that the skull is formed from the fusion of segments must be rejected.

Part iv. of " The Principles of Biology " deals with Physiological Development, and proceeds on lines very similar to those just described in the case of Morphological Development. Much of it indeed might have been included under that heading; for, as functions cannot be studied apart from their corresponding structures, the exposition must be largely founded upon the development of structure. The main purpose of the argument is to show that functions, like structures, are evolved as a result of the external forces acting upon the organism.

As already pointed out, the most primitive organisms, both animal and plant, are comparatively homogeneous throughout, and every part of their body is capable of performing every function necessary to their existence. Incident forces, however, soon break up this aboriginal

homogeneity ; for (as shown in " First Principles ")
they must act differently on different parts of the
organism. Very early in evolution there is thus
established a differentiation between the exterior
and interior of an organism, for it is here that the
incident forces differ most widely. The difference
between exterior and interior remains throughout
evolution one of the most important manifestations of heterogeneity, whether we consider it in
a single cell with its cytoplasm and cell-wall,
or in a forest tree, in which the exterior of the stem
becomes modified to form bark. The fixed and the
free ends of plants are widely different, because
the forces which act upon them are widely different.
Fishes, swimming in a medium which acts uniformly on every side, are nevertheless more exposed
to the action of light from above than from below ;
and this difference in external forces has set up a
difference of colour between their superior and
inferior surfaces. Very numerous instances are
cited in further substantiation of the same doctrine.

The origin of the vascular system in plants is
then discussed. As their stems sway backwards
and forwards in the wind, the sap will be squeezed
at intervals out of some parts into others. It will
tend to move in the direction where the resistance
is least, and, constantly moving along the same
channels, will necessarily give rise by ordinary
mechanics to just that system which is actually

found. These paths are gradually cleared and made definite by constant use ; and their permanency in future generations will be ensured by inheritance of the effects thus gradually brought about. Spencer even makes the suggestion that the blood-vessels of animals have originated in a similar manner.

The general result of Spencer's whole discussion is this :—Every structure and every function of an animal or plant is moulded gradually in the course of evolution by the forces of its environment. Where equal forces have acted equally on different parts of an organism, those parts will be similar both in structure and in function. Where forces act unequally, the structures and functions will be different, and the greater the inequality the greater the difference. Spencer reaches the conclusions, therefore, that the environment modifies any individual organism by direct action upon it : the modification thus wrought is perpetuated by heredity, and is increased from generation to generation by continued action of the environment in the same sense, till at length there are evolved the actual structures and functions of animals and plants as we know them. Those structures, such as the mammalian skull, which never can have been produced by any direct forces are explained by reference to natural selection.

The last division of " The Principles of Biology " deals with the Laws of Multiplication. The propagation and spread of species depend upon the balance preserved between two antagonistic sets of factors. One set of factors tends towards the extinction of species—namely, natural death, enemies, lack of food, atmospheric changes, etc. The other set of factors tends towards the increase of species—namely, the endurance, strength, swiftness, and sagacity of its members, as also their fertility. In a species which is not becoming extinct, the fertility must be sufficient to counterbalance the forces of destruction; and the demands consequently made upon the reproductive powers of a species must vary inversely as the power of self-preservation possessed by its individuals. That is to say, if individuals have small power of self-preservation, if there is a large wastage of life, or, in other words, a high mortality, there must be a high fertility in compensation. If both fertility and individual power of self-preservation were highly developed, the species would quickly multiply to a prohibitive extent: it would be confronted by famine, disease, or enemies, which would quickly reduce the power of individual self-preservation. If, on the other hand, this power were already low, and there was no compensating fertility, the species would become extinct. There must exist, therefore, on

à priori grounds, an *antagonism between individuation and reproduction.* Spencer then goes on to
show that such antagonism actually exists.

The size of an animal or plant is one index
of the extent to which its individuality is developed.
And, in general, the largest animals and plants
reproduce the most slowly, while the smallest
reproduce with the greatest rapidity. Minute
organisms like Bacteria can multiply a millionfold
in a few hours ; moreover, their reproduction
is largely asexual. The lowest kind of organisms
reproduce simply by dividing in two, or by growing out buds which then drop off and become new
individuals. The highest kind, on the other hand,
invariably reproduce sexually. The same antagonism between growth and genesis is observed
in species where reproduction is exclusively sexual.
Small birds lay more eggs than large birds ; an
oak produces fewer acorns in the course of several
centuries than a fungus does spores in a single
night ; a rotifer may lay fifty eggs within a week
or two, whereas an elephant lives thirty years
before it gives birth to a single young one. The
inverse relation between fertility and growth is
paralleled by an inverse relation between fertility
and the activity or energy spent by an animal :
it is those animals which spend least energy in
locomotion, or heat-maintenance, or otherwise,
that reproduce with the greatest rapidity.

On the other hand, reproduction or genesis is directly proportional to the amount of nutrition. Animals and plants which receive abundant nutrition are correspondingly fertile. It is true that fatness hinders fertility in domestic animals; but this is because the fat is in reality a product of degeneration rather than any addition to the individuality of the animal. Spencer cites many instances to show that where individuals have much to eat and little to do they are highly fertile; but where they have much to do and little to eat they are comparatively barren. The general antagonism between genesis and reproduction is, however, to be qualified by the statement that genesis decreases not quite so fast as individuation increases.

The operation of this same law is traced by Spencer in the multiplication of the human species. Men are relatively fertile in districts where food is abundant and work moderate. The Cape Boers and the French Canadians are cited in illustration of very fecund races, which have abundance of food and a small output of physical and mental labour. The popular belief that highly-fed men are comparatively infertile is erroneous, except in so far as the feeding may give rise to fat and " abnormal plethora." The future of the human race is then considered. Evolution will probably proceed along the lines of a higher intellectual, and still more of a higher moral, development. The main factor of advancing evolution is the excess of fertility; and it is to be anticipated that this fertility will decline as the capacities of individuals increase. At length there will be reached a time when equilibrium will be almost attained. Man will have reached so high a stage of individuation that his fertility will be diminished to such a point that no excess of population is brought into the world. His high emotional and intellectual development will cause him to feel the ordinary duties of life as pleasurable: there will be nothing laborious in his existence; and the main factor of discomfort (over-rapidity of breeding) will have disappeared. Yet this happy state of ultimate equilibrium can never be entirely attained. For the gradual changes of the environment will ever introduce new disturbances, which will have to be met by corresponding modifications of the race. With this theory Spencer brings his " Principles of Biology " to an end.

CHAPTER XI

PSYCHOLOGY

SPENCER's Psychology is most nearly related to the Associationist School. His "Principles of Psychology" is a work of the highest originality; though we are apt in these days to lose sight of that fact, owing to the circumstance that so many of his leading ideas have become incorporated into the common knowledge of the times. Its leading and most original feature, perhaps, is the treatment of psychology from the standpoint of evolution. Spencer further showed true scientific insight in basing the work on a careful study of the structure and functions of the nervous system. It is unnecessary to follow him through "The Data of Psychology," which merely furnishes a singularly lucid account of the functions of the nervous system in so far as they were known at the time when he wrote. He bestows the title of "Aestho-Physiology" on the study of the relation between mental and nervous phenomena, and endeavoured with remarkable perspicacity to show that feeling and nervous activity were two sides of the same thing.

"The Inductions of Biology" enters into an

inquiry as to the nature of the substance of which mind is composed, and the conclusion is reached that the problem is insoluble. We can decompose mind into the various elements of which it is built up : we can say that it consists of emotions, intelligence, etc. ; but we cannot say what it *is*, in its ultimate nature, any more than we can say what matter is.

When we analyse mental processes or (as Spencer always calls them) feelings, we find reason to believe that they are compounded from certain elementary units. A sudden sound produces a mild and instantaneous shock ; and from some such unit of mental action Spencer supposes that all feelings (including sensations, emotions, etc.) are built up. In the case of musical sound, we know that this is so. A rapid succession of taps are, if they are not too rapid, perceived as a series of individual sounds. When the speed is increased to more than sixteen a second, they cease to be individually distinguishable and become blended together to form a musical tone. By further blending of different tones differences of *timbre* are produced. While auditory sensations are thus shown to be compounded from multitudes of single units, variously arranged as regards coexistence and sequence, we may assume that *all* sensations, whether of sight, smell, etc., are produced in a similar way ; and in fact that the basis of all feeling consists in some single unit or unspecialised shock, and that the numberless different variations in the quality and intensity of feeling are due to differences in the way this elementary unit is compounded—in the different systems of coexistence and sequence into which it is woven.

Passing from the ultimate composition of mind to its proximate composition, Spencer finds it to consist of two main kinds of components—Feelings, and Relations between Feelings. A feeling is "any portion of consciousness which occupies a place sufficiently large to give it a perceivable individuality; which has its individuality marked off from adjacent portions of consciousness by qualitative contrasts; and which, when introspectively contemplated, appears to be homogeneous." A relation between feelings, on the other hand, is characterised by occupying no appreciable part of consciousness.

Feelings are further subdivided into the two main categories of emotions and sensations, the former being centrally initiated and the latter peripherally initiated. Sensations, again, are divisible into those initiated at the ends of nerves on the outer surface of the body and those initiated at the ends of nerves distributed within the body. The class of feelings may be divided otherwise into those that are vivid and those that are faint.

The vivid or primary feelings are those corresponding to Hume's "impressions"; the faint or secondary feelings are those that correspond to "ideas."

Relations between feelings may be analysed into the detection of differences between two successive feelings. Relations between feelings last no appreciable time, and consist purely in the recognition of the amount of likeness or unlikeness between any feeling and that which immediately succeeds it in the mind. Relations between feelings, moreover (when the feelings are recognised as dissimilar), fall into one or other of the two main categories of coexistence or sequence. The recognition of simultaneity or succession is characteristic of relations between feelings.

Consciousness of the emotional type is widely different from consciousness of the sensational type, the difference consisting of the larger or smaller proportions of the relational elements present. Emotions are vaguely marked off from one another, and have few and indefinite relations. Sensations, on the other hand—those, at least, initiated on the surface of the body—are characterised by abundance of sharp and definite relations. Objects seen by the eye set up impressions of colour, whose mutual limitations are sharp and numerous. Sounds in the same way are separated from each other by clear and precise demarcations.

Further distinctions are then drawn between emotion and sensation. Sensation readily enters into association; emotion does not. Sensations can be easily recalled; emotions cannot; and so on. All this probably constitutes the most philosophic presentation of the associationist school; and it is needless to go into the details of it.

The " General " and " Special " Syntheses are the next two divisions of " The Principles of Psychology." The " General Synthesis " has already been referred to in the previous chapter. It defines Life as the correspondence between inner and outer relations. The " Special Synthesis " carries the same theory into a purely psychological sphere. But the main importance of this part resides in Spencer's attempted reconciliation between Transcendentalism and Empiricism. Locke and the Empirical School affirmed that intelligence was exclusively based upon the results of experience accumulated within the life of the individual. Kant and the Transcendental School affirmed, on the contrary, that intelligence was a natural endowment à *priori*, and had little or nothing to do with experience. Spencer took up the position that each party had seen one side of the truth. He said that every individual *inherits* from its predecessors the results of their experience, and thus starts upon a higher level than they did. In every individual the growth of experience has its counterpart in structural modifications and development of the nervous system : those structural modifications acquired during the individuals' life are handed down by heredity to its posterity, which thus commences life at a higher level of intelligence than its predecessors. Spencer held that Locke was right in saying that all intelligence is derived from experience, but it is the experience, not of the individual, but of the race. It was equally true, as Kant said, that intelligence is largely preordained as regards the individual; but that prearranged disposition is not transcendental in character—it is the accumulated result of the experience of former generations. According to Spencer, therefore, intelligence is *à priori* as regards the individual and *à posteriori* as regards the race.

This theory has had a considerable vogue. But unfortunately it is based, again, on the belief that acquired characters may be inherited. It has a neatness and conciliatory aspect that is immensely attractive to most minds; but it is a mere piece of imagination—a theory not only unsupported by facts, but in opposition to the direction in which the available facts appear to lead. Instinct is explained by Spencer on the same principle—as acquirements that have become hereditary. He imagined that instinctive animal actions were originally intelligent. Among ourselves we know that things laboriously learnt, such as playing the piano, become after a time easy and as it were instinctive. It becomes possible to play off a tune while thinking of quite different things. In the same way, Spencer supposed that all instincts among animals were at first acquired by a laborious experience of their ancestry : that with each successive generation the actions became easier, until at length they became pure instinct requiring no thought or intelligence whatever. This theory, again, scarcely needs comment ; it is now almost unanimously rejected by biologists.

A far more scientific theory on the part of Spencer was that in which he regarded instinct as compound reflex action, and reason as a still more compound process of instinct. This belief is now tolerably well established. Spencer's error is only as to the relative order in which reflex action, instinct, and reason first appeared. He represented reason (or experience) as coming first in evolution. It gradually settled down in numerous often-repeated actions to instinct ; and finally the instinct assumed the purely automatic form of reflex action. But in point of fact evolution has proceeded in the opposite direction. Reflex action came first, then instinct, and last of all intelligence. Nor could it have come about in the way that Spencer suggested ; the perpetual repetition of one act during an individual's lifetime does undoubtedly lead to a sort of instinctive facility, but that acquired facility shows no tendency to reappear in subsequent generations, which have each to learn these same acts from the beginning with as much labour as their predecessors. This result, so contrary to expectation, has emerged after long researches by biologists. It is small blame to Spencer that, in the middle of last century, he had failed to recognise it.

Spencer next turns to what he calls the " Physical Synthesis," which is in reality a hypothesis as to the origin of the nervous system. Assuming the earliest forms of animal life to consist of undifferentiated specks of protoplasm, in which an external stimulus is immediately followed by contraction, a stage is reached at which a stimulus is habitually experienced at some point of the surface of the animal—its tentacles, for instance— and spreads a wave of molecular change throughout the organism. But as a result of differences of composition in the different parts the wave will travel more readily in some directions than in others ; and contractions will therefore occur more readily in those directions. The fundamental law is that a wave of molecular motion travelling along a particular path facilitates the passage of subsequent waves along the same path, just as water running over sand does not spread evenly over it, but cuts out a number of sharply-defined channels leaving the intermediate spaces dry. So there will after a time be set up in the undifferentiated protoplasm channels of easy communication between certain parts. Starting from a point subject to frequent external stimulus, waves of molecular motion will tend always more insistently to pursue definite channels instead of being dissipated at large throughout the organism. The terminal points of these channels will mark the portions of the animal which contract in consequence of the stimulus. Now since this acquired modification in the permeability of the protoplasm is, according to Spencer, inherited, each generation will derive from its parents a body which is already endowed with paths of easy communication. As these paths become always more definite with each generation, and as the general protoplasm loses its conductivity in the same proportion, we may at length expect to find strands of specially adapted protoplasm spreading through the animal's body. We have, in fact, a mechanical theory of the genesis of nerves.

All this is extremely ingenious and in great part true. It is vitiated to some extent by the fallacy, already pointed out, of supposing that instinct is inherited habit. Spencer defends his theory from the charge of materialism by saying that the intimate nature of mind remains entirely inexplicable and wholly different from the intimate nature of matter. If none the less his theory appears to us materialistic, it is certainly not more so than many of the later developments of nervous physiology.

We pass now to the second volume of " The Principles of Psychology," and to that division of the work entitled " Special Analysis." We are here concerned only with intellectual operations ; feeling is expressly excluded from the purview of the " Special Analysis," for sentiments and feelings offer no prospect of successful analysis. The " Special Analysis " begins with the highest type of intellectual operation and gradually works down to the simplest. The highest type is described as compound quantitative reasoning, and the following is an example of it.

An engineer who has constructed a tubular bridge is required to construct another of the same kind, but double the span. It might be imagined that he would simply have to magnify the previous design in all particulars ; but this would be inadequate. For whereas the weight of the bridge varies as the *cubes* of the linear dimensions, its power of resistance increases only with the *squares* of the linear dimensions. If, therefore, all the linear dimensions were merely doubled, the weight of the bridge would be increased by a greater ratio than its supporting power, and it would collapse.

This intellectual operation consists in the detection of an inequality between two relations. The first relation is that between the sustaining forces of the first and second bridge, and is represented by $1^2 : 2^2$. The second is that between the destroying forces, and is represented by $1^3 : 2^3$. It is in the perception of the difference between these two ratios that the mental act of the engineer consists; and the instance is to be regarded as typical of all reasoning. Expressed in an abstract form, the process is an application of the axiom—ratios (or relations) which are severally equal to certain other ratios that are unequal to each other are themselves unequal. In the same way we reach the axiom that relations which are equal to the same relation are equal to one another; and upon this axiom is based the whole of mathematical analysis, together with important parts of geometry. Compound quantitative reasoning consists, then, in a succession of steps, each of which may be regarded as the statement of an equality between two relations. The recognition of equality or inequality between relations is the basis to which all reasoning may be reduced by analysis. It is moreover a direct mental intuition. The process by which the mind perceives the identity or the difference of two relations is ultimate and axiomatic; it is not capable of any still more minute analysis.

Quantitative reasoning in general involves three ideas—coextension, coexistence, and connature. That is to say, each step in the reasoning process is concerned with two terms : and of these terms it asserts *either* that they occupy or do not occupy equal spaces (coextension) ; *or* that they occur or do not occur at the same time (coexistence) ; *or* that they are or are not of the same kind (connature). The intuition underlying all quantitative reasoning consists in a perception of the equality of two magnitudes. The most simple form of quantitative reasoning arises when the equality of these two magnitudes is *inferred* from the fact that they are each equal to some third magnitude. The introduction of further magnitudes is the source of further complication, so that in an ultimate analysis all quantitative reasoning is reduced to the recognition of equality or inequality between two relations.

Qualitative reasoning differs from quantitative reasoning by omission of the factor of coextension. Instead of predicating equality between two relations in Space, Time, and Quality, we predicate it only in Time and Quality. Quantitative reasoning proceeds by a comparison of the *quantity* of certain existences of determinate quality. Qualitative reasoning, on the other hand, proceeds by a comparison of the *quality* of certain determinate existences, or by an examination of the coexistence of certain determinate *qualities*. The kind of reasoning commonly embodied in the syllogism is of this type. But the syllogism itself is, according to Spencer, an erroneous representation of the true method of reasoning. It is erroneous in that it expressly includes a major premise in the process ; and in actual fact we do not usually in our mental operations refer back to the major premise. Take for instance the syllogism

> " All men are mortal.
> Socrates is a man,
> therefore
> Socrates is mortal."

But in point of fact we do not in thought go back to the proposition that " all men are mortal." The value of the syllogism is not as explanatory of the actual process of reasoning, but as testing the method by which the conclusion has been reached—by forcing us to recognise the full implications of our statements. From perfect qualitative reasoning we pass to imperfect qualitative reasoning. This is characterised by the fact that relations are no longer considered as equal or unequal, but as like or unlike. This holds of that kind of syllogistic reasoning in which there is a considerable difference between the subjects of the major and minor premise, so that the argument is more or less one of analogy. It also applies to inductive reasoning, or reasoning from particulars to generals, as well from particulars to particulars.

Classification, naming, and recognition are obviously intellectual processes which consist in the perception of a resemblance between external things or relations. A newly-discovered animal is referred to the class of mammals if it presents characters like those which are distinctive of mammals. The perception of external objects depends upon the same process. The immediate sensations derived from an external object have a resemblance to previous sensations which are associated with the idea of the object in question.

The perception of Space is derived from experience of matter. All matter is presented to us as extended in form : by abstraction we attain the idea of empty space. Space, being a universal form of the *non-ego*, inevitably generates a corresponding universal form of the *ego*. Space becomes known from the coexistence of two or more separate spots, and is thus founded upon a relation between at least two elements of consciousness. The idea of Time is similarly derived from an experience of *successive* states of consciousness ; and is therefore founded upon a perception of the *difference* between two states. The idea of time is an abstract of all relations of position among successive states of consciousness.

Various forms of relations are next considered ;

and they are all found to be reducible by analysis to the recognition of *likeness* or *unlikeness* between two terms. When the likeness between the two compared terms rises to indistinguishableness, it is called Equality. Likeness and unlikeness are known only by the fact that a change in consciousness does or does not occur. On passing from one term to another, either no change of consciousness is experienced—in which case there is a judgment of likeness; or some change is experienced—in which case there is a judgment of unlikeness. All intellectual operations therefore depend upon the occurrence of some change in the sequence of consciousness. If consciousness continued without change, it would be equivalent to no consciousness at all. Thinking is "relationing"; its only basis is the recognition of similarity or dissimilarity between two successive states of consciousness. With this conclusion, the "Special Analysis" comes to an end.

There still remain two divisions of Spencer's Psychology which demand attention. The first of these is entitled "Congruities." It passes in review the doctrines previously established in the course of the work, pointing out the harmony existing among them. A comparison is instituted between nervous and mental phenomena, with a view to showing their parallelism. If mind consists of feelings and the relations between feelings, the nervous system consists of nerve-cells and of fibres which place them in communication with one another. Both mental and nervous processes may be analysed into a succession of rapid pulses : each is based upon a single unit of function ; and in each the developed whole is built out of these units compounded and re-compounded with one another in innumerable different ways. The laws of association in thought are shown to be paralleled by the structure of the nervous system, etc. Numerous other congruities are mentioned before we are once again brought round to the doctrine of Transfigured Realism.

The final division of " The Principles of Psychology " deals with the *Corollaries* flowing from the body of the work. It is preparatory to the succeeding portions of the Philosophy, dealing with Sociology and Ethics ; and in modern times it would be described as Social Psychology. First we are introduced to a classification of mental faculties. The primary division (as already stated) is into feelings and the relations between feelings, or, in more ordinary language, into feelings and cognitions. Each of these main groups is further sub-divisible according to degrees of abstractness. Dealing first with *cognitions*, we have " Presentative Cognitions," the most concrete of all, in which consciousness is occupied simply in localising a sensation impressed on the organism. Next come " Presentative-Representative Cognitions," in which consciousness is occupied with the relation between an immediate sensation and the associated ideas formed through previous experience. This corresponds to Perception. Thirdly, we have " Representative Cognitions," corresponding to memory ; and lastly " Re-representative Cognitions," in which past ideas are not merely reproduced, but combined in new forms, as in imagination or abstract thought.

Feelings are subdivided in a parallel manner. " Presentative Feelings " are Sensation, from the point of view merely of pleasure or pain, without any intellectual ingredient. " Presentative-Representative Feelings " are those in which an immediate sensation is associated with emotions derived from a vast aggregate of previously-experienced sensations. " Representative Feelings " are those in which there is no present external stimulus ; these include the emotions which consist of aggregated ideas of previously-experienced sensations. " Re-representative Feelings " include the higher sentiments, such as the love of property, justice, and liberty. These are built up from great aggregates of elementary sensations. Take, for instance, the sentiment of love of freedom. In isolated cases, previously experienced, restriction has involved pain. A painful sensation in many instances may be arrested by making

certain movements—away from the source of
pain, for example. The feeling of repugnance to
pain therefore becomes associated with any circumstances which prohibit the necessary movements. By generalisation from a great number of
such cases there ultimately becomes established
a sentiment in favour of freedom in the abstract.
Such a sentiment is a re-representative feeling.

The language of the emotions is then dealt with.
Emotion is always accompanied by a powerful
nervous discharge, and this leads to muscular
movement. In pain, for instance, the vocal
organs, being the smallest, are moved first, and
cries are given out. As the pain increases all the
muscles in the body may become involved. In
addition to a *diffused* nervous discharge, there is
a *restricted* nervous discharge for each separate
emotion. This discharge is an incipient activity
of the muscles which would be set in motion by the
act to which the emotion leads. Thus a car-
nivorous animal in eating its prey has to retract
its lips and uncover its teeth. The act of snarling
is simply this preliminary ; and the mental
expression of anger is nothing else than the
incipient movement of those muscles which would
be used in devouring the prey.

Surveying Spencer's Psychology as a whole,
we cannot but be struck with the magnitude and
brilliance of its conceptions. It is unquestionably

what is called an epoch-making work. It introduced the idea of evolution into the science of psychology ; and this fact is the more remarkable when we remember that " The Principles of Psychology " was first published four years before the appearance of " The Origin of Species." To this circumstance, however, is due the inherent weakness of many parts of the work. Spencer based evolution throughout on the inheritance of acquired characters : in the main doctrines there is no attempt to utilise natural selection. Hence, while he was usually right in his main evolutionary propositions, he was wrong in the details. If the book had been based upon natural selection, it would probably have been the most remarkable philosophic production of last century. As it is, Spencer's Psychology is of the first importance in the history of the subject ; and even now is far better worth reading than the great majority of text-books which have been produced since his time. For the general point of view and the general method are quite beyond criticism : it is only minor points that have been affected by the progress of knowledge.

CHAPTER XII

EDUCATION

SPENCER's little volume on Education is almost the only one of his works that has been recognised by the official world. More than any other single text-book it is the foundation of all the so-called "modern" ideas in education. To anyone ignorant of Spencer's methods, it would appear highly surprising that this classical work should have been written by a man not yet forty, who had had only two or three months' experience of teaching, who was unmarried and had come into very little contact with children. But the achievement is typical of Spencer's methods. His principles were always *à priori;* the verification of them by practical experience came afterwards. If in the present work and in his "Psychology" he succeeded in formulating new theories of great importance and interest, his success was in neither case due to preliminary study or knowledge, but to a happy instinct which guided him safely in these difficult subjects.

The first question he discusses, with regard to education, is "What knowledge is of most worth?" He points out that the choice of

subjects which may be taught to a child is almost
unlimited ; and nearly all of these subjects will
be of some value to it in adult life. But since the
actual amount that can be learnt is strictly
limited, it becomes a question of selecting from
the various possible subjects those which will
be of greatest value subsequently. From this
utilitarian point of view Spencer reaches the
conclusion that science is of far greater value than
any other subject whatever. The most important
information that can be imparted concerns the
maintenance of life and good health : hence the
elements of hygiene and physiology are the first
essentials. The next necessity is for success in
earning a livelihood. Spencer enumerates many
instances to show the failure which occurs in
business owing to ignorance of science ; and he
infers that the most valuable knowledge as a
foundation for practical life is an acquaintance
with the natural properties of objects — the
elements of physics and other sciences. The next
necessity for the adult is to fit himself for the duties
and responsibilities of parentage ; and for this
purpose psychology and education should be
studied. After the duties of the family come
those of the State : the child should be prepared
to play its part in the government of the country,
and should be taught the rudiments of the social
sciences in order that the future man may be in

a position to cast a well-informed and intelligent vote. Spencer points out, moreover, that in time of war a knowledge of science may be the turning-point of the national safety. It may be noted, however, that he does not inculcate the teaching of patriotism. In his time nationality was far less developed than it is now.

Lastly, Spencer expresses the view that one of the highest enjoyments of life is in art of all forms. The final essential of a good education, therefore, is a training in the appreciation of art ; and it is rather surprising to find that here also the first requisite is a knowledge of science. Spencer cites instances of technical errors in the works of well-known painters, and shows how these errors are due to ignorance of the properties of light, or of perspective ; and he concludes that scientific knowledge is the true basis of æsthetic appreciation. He is perhaps on stronger ground when he affirms that science is itself an art, and that it cultivates a certain kind of artistic instinct in those who most tenaciously pursue it.

From the question of the utilitarian value of different kinds of knowledge he turns to the effect of each kind on mental development, or to its value as mental training or discipline. Here once again he finds that science has a greater value than any other kind of knowledge. He deprecates the learning of dead languages, and considers that the acquirement of languages in general is a far less useful intellectual discipline than the study of science. He condemns rote-learning altogether, as being entirely mechanical and divorced from the exercise of intelligence. Science alone fully develops the intellectual faculties; and he points out that as an exercise for memory it is at least as efficient as learning a language. Languages and rote-learning have the further important disadvantage that they are purely arbitrary and given by authority without making any appeal to reason. Science, on the other hand, abhors authority. The child is told almost nothing *ex cathedrâ;* it learns direct for itself from Nature by means of observation and experiment. It comes thus to know how things actually hang together in the world; it learns to reason, and to judge and to find out things for itself. Not only from the utilitarian point of view, therefore, but also as a mental discipline, Spencer concludes that the study of science should be the pre-eminent ingredient in a good education.

Since he wrote this work (at the end of the 'fifties), his views on the subject have gained a popularity which must then have seemed almost impossible. Science has been everywhere introduced into general education, and each year sees an extension of the principle and a demand always for more science in our schools. If the present movement continues, we shall in time attain the realisation of Spencer's ideas. Whether or not we think them sound is still largely a matter of personal constitution.

There are many now who hold that Spencer's exaltation of scientific training is rational and wise, so long as science is well taught. Bad teaching, in their opinion, may counterbalance every advantage claimed for science, and may introduce into it a dullness and irrationality much exceeding that of languages. And they go on to argue that, so long as teaching is a poorly paid profession, it cannot on the average be very good: and hence that in practice science does not have the great advantages which it might have under a more theoretically perfect *régime*.

It is pointed out, moreover, that, as regards utility in after life, many living languages have a far greater value than Spencer was prepared to admit. Children's minds are very different; and Spencer's theories are plainly those which would have been most suitable to his own mind. That these ideals should be the goal of a large part of public education seems indubitable; but universality is a hard word, and it may very well be that a purely scientific education would not be the best training for *all* minds. These questions, however, are for the expert, and to be settled by an appeal to experience. The chief point for us

to note is that Spencer was the pioneer of the
modern movement.

His next chapter deals with intellectual education; and here also modern fashion is largely
due to his work. He carried a step farther the
principles of Pestalozzi, and expunged many of
the pioneer crudities of that reformer. His
methods showed, indeed, a strong affinity with
those expressed in a more primitive form in
Rousseau's " Emile "—a work, however, which
he never read. He lays down a certain number of
general maxims. Education should lead from the
simple to the complex; from the indefinite to
the definite. Grammar, for instance, should be
the last and not the first study in the acquisition
of a language. In every sphere precision is not to
be expected in a young child; it is a later development, and the teacher should be content at first
with the inculcation of rough and crude conceptions, without aiming at accuracy or detail.
Education should proceed from the concrete to
the abstract—an idea which has now been widely
adopted on the Kindergarten principle. The
order in which subjects should be taught as the
child grows up should be the same order as that in
which knowledge was gradually acquired by the
human race. The mind of the child is like the
mind of primitive man; and the succession of
human discoveries provides a true index to the

order in which the various subjects should follow
one another.

The next principle is that education should lead
from the empirical to the rational. All knowledge
imparted should at first begin with observations
and experiments by the child itself. General
laws and principles should be allowed slowly to
grow up from this experimental basis, and should
on no account be taught from the beginning.
Children should always be encouraged to work
on their own initiative, to find out as much as
possible for themselves, and to be told as little
as possible by other people. Spencer's final test
of a good education is whether it creates a pleasurable excitement in the pupils. Knowledge gathered
under the stimulus of interest and pleasure is a
permanent possession. That which excites only
dislike and boredom is soon lost; and the dislike
itself is evidence that the child's mind is still
unripe for that particular subject. Needless to
say, the success of any such scheme presupposes
a high degree of intelligence in the teacher; but
that is a drawback of all advanced systems of
education, and Spencer very truly observes that
the indifference of teachers is no argument against
the validity of the principles themselves, though
it may be against the universal application of them.

Spencer next proceeds to a study of moral education. He does not advocate the express incul-

cation of moral maxims (we have already seen that
he did not propose to teach patriotism). His
view was that moral education should work
through the feelings and sentiments rather than
through the intellect ; and he was certainly right,
according to more recent studies, in his opinion
that morals are based on feeling and not on knowledge or intellect. With regard to punishments,
his general principle was that they should, to as
small an extent as possible, be meted out by
parents or teachers in an arbitrary fashion ; but
that reliance should be placed upon the natural
discipline of consequences. Take for instance the
case of unpunctuality : it is a mistake to allot
a particular penalty to this offence. The natural
punishment of unpunctuality in ordinary life is
that of missing the advantages derived from
keeping time. Hence, when the child is late for
any amusement or play which it expected, it should
be excluded from participation. Again, if it shows
a tendency to play with lighted matches, and
disregards warning, it should not be commanded
imperatively with threats to desist. The mother
should take care to be about when it is so engaged,
that there may be no serious damage ; and the
punishment of burning its fingers will be far more
effective than arbitrary chastisement, as well as
lead to a greater faith in future warnings instead
of to an attitude of hostility between parent and

child. But of course Spencer allows that there are limits beyond which this principle (now so well recognised) cannot be applied.

Spencer does not suggest that a child should never be punished by its parents. On the contrary, when it has knowingly acted contrary to their wishes, it is part of the natural consequences that they should be temporarily less well-disposed towards it than usual. Punishment of this kind should be of a negative rather than positive character. It should not take the form of chastisement, but rather of withholding benefits or manifestations of affection. Just as, in adult life, wrong actions bring their own punishment, so in child life the best form of moral education is that which proceeds on the same principle. And even that should not be applied too harshly. In harmony with its low physical and intellectual development a child has a low moral development; and too much should not be required from it. Moral precocity is as undesirable as intellectual precocity. Commands should seldom be issued, but when they are issued the most rigorous obedience should be exacted. But the *régime* of command and obedience is false; the child should be taught to govern itself rather than to acquiesce in being governed. In the world it will have to look after itself, form its own judgments, and control its own conduct. That end is not attained by the habit of deferring always to the authority of others.

Lastly Spencer points out that as a rule the treatment of children is determined by the mere approbation or annoyance of the moment, instead of by a methodical system. Education is a highly complex art, demanding exceptional qualities in teachers. And Spencer rightly perceived that the first essential of a good teacher is the capacity for sympathising with the child's mind and discerning its various thoughts and motives. The principles which he formulated are intended to be those natural to a teacher of high sympathetic powers : no principles are of any avail to a teacher who lacks these powers; in such a case we have merely the form without the substance of a good education. Doubtless this is sufficient reason why most people may find these, as also any other principles, disappointing in their results.

Finally Spencer deals with Physical Education, a branch of the subject to which he attached great importance. He repeats what we now regard as a time-honoured fallacy, that the younger generation are physically inferior to the old, that they are lower in stature, and tend to be degenerate physically. It is curious how this same fallacy is endemic and permanent in all ages. In England it appears regularly in the writings of every period since Gildas wrote his " De excidio Britanniæ " in the sixth century. It was entertained by Shakespeare and many poets. It was taken up by the philosopher Berkeley in his " Essay towards preventing the Ruin of Great Britain." John Stuart Mill committed himself in the same way, and here we see Spencer expressing again the old fallacy. But he unfortunately attempted to explain it by reference to newer fallacies. He speaks of a lady of robust parentage, who as a result of under-feeding and over-working developed an enfeebled constitution, which her children had inherited from her. Few biologists will allow the possibility of such an occurrence. Nevertheless, Spencer was undoubtedly right in the main outlines of his physical education, and his ideas here as elsewhere have been very generally adopted. The criticism which he made upon the physical education of his time was that it erred by deficient feeding, deficient clothing, deficient exercise (at least among girls), and excessive mental application. As regards feeding, he refers to the alternating tendencies to give either too much or too little, and insists that the best guide is in the promptings of the child itself. When its natural feelings have not been perverted by surfeiting or by withholding particular kinds of food, it knows better what it needs than its instructors can. Spencer very strongly condemns excessive mental application at an early age.

Certainly he was free from any such forcing himself ; and his own education furnishes a curious contrast to the intensive system applied to John Stuart Mill. Yet though the milder system may have the majority of advantages, the severe methods do bring out certain qualities which we find in Mill but not in Spencer. In his philosophy Mill was usually prepared to face a disagreeable conclusion if logic compelled him to it ; Spencer was not. Severity bestows a tinge of asceticism, which in many philosophical studies is a valuable mental trait.

Thus we see that Spencer's education, like Rousseau's, aimed at being a natural system. It reflected his own personal character, and was no doubt well suited to him individually. It was all part of his unified system of thought. The central idea was liberty, and the main objections were to any form of compulsion. The child, like the nation, was to be freed from over-government. Government in fact was to be reduced to the smallest possible sphere. His ideas have been widely adopted in education, but scarcely at all in politics. Yet it is the case that the arguments are sometimes identical in both spheres. In education, for instance, it is well known that truth-telling and freedom are associated together ; while coercive methods are almost invariably associated with lying. The fact is derivative from the foundations of human nature itself; and Spencer believed the same relation to subsist in communities of men. But education, complex as it is, is far less complex than politics. In a couple of decades the child has grown up, and long before then the results of education may be observed. In society effects follow causes at a far longer interval, and we should probably have to substitute generations for decades in the preceding statement. Moreover, a child is permanently under control and observation; it is far more plastic and modifiable than a society. Education makes or unmakes it far more easily than government can make or unmake a nation. Still it is true that in both cases it is human nature that we have to deal with; and a society or a crowd has many resemblances to a child. It is impulsive, cruel, emotional, and stupid. Its moral consciousness, its intellectual capacities, its capacity for self-restraint are much below those of the average individual composing it. But, however we may view these subjects, it is beyond question that Spencer's educational ideas sprang from the same mental peculiarities as those which gave birth to his social and political principles.

CHAPTER XIII

CONCLUSION

It was one of the cardinal maxims of " First Principles " that all motion is rhythmical in character. Among the numerous illustrations which Spencer cited in favour of this belief is the movement of public opinion with regard to popular authors. He pointed out that the judgment of men tended to fluctuate between excessive admiration and excessive depreciation : it did not maintain an even level. The illustration is at all events very forcibly brought before us by his own case. In the 'seventies and 'eighties of last century his reputation was at its height. His name produced an almost magical effect in many social circles. He was the fashionable philosopher of the time. He summed up the spirit of the age more accurately than any other writer.

Within a quarter of a century, however, an immense change of public opinion had taken place. On the scientific side the doctrine of Evolution with which his name was so largely associated had been accepted by nearly everyone, and had ceased to be a matter of current controversy. Moreover, the mode of evolution which had found favour among men of science was not that which Spencer advocated. The belief in the inheritance of acquired characters was generally condemned; and the other factor—that of Natural Selection—was associated with the name of Darwin rather than that of Spencer. In 1900, also, the new movement in Biology began, which relegated even natural selection to quite a secondary place in the thoughts of men of science. Of the other principles of his Biology and Psychology many had come to be taken as part of common knowledge; and from being highly original suggestions had degenerated into platitudes. Other principles, again, had been condemned; and the remainder had passed for a time out of the arena of public attention.

On the social side an even greater change had come about. Spencer stood for peace and individual liberty; and both these ideals had suffered a grave decline in public favour. In so far as liberty was concerned, the chief infractions of it which had existed at the beginning of the century had been abolished; and political movements travelled along new lines, wholly opposed to Spencer's teaching. And as regards war, the country was plunged in the midst of the fight with the Boer Republics; the military spirit was growing, and was fostered by circumstances. The Imperialist and Protectionist agitations were both in deep opposition to every sentiment of Spencer's mind ; and he uttered his opinions with characteristic force and disregard of all opposition.

Accordingly, when the present century opened, he found himself one of the most unpopular public men in England. His death evoked indeed a chorus of praise in the newspapers ; but mainly, it is to be feared, from journalists who had found no opportunity of studying his views. *The Times*, on the other hand, published an attack upon him, which in those days was very strongly worded even for that journal of uncompromising beliefs.

Notwithstanding the long notices of his death in the newspapers, it was widely felt that the English people as a whole did not adequately realise how great a personality had passed from among them. Comment was made on the fact that in many foreign countries his death was more deeply mourned than in his own country : in Italy, for instance, the Chamber immediately adjourned when the announcement of Spencer's death was made, and in France there were many criticisms upon the comparative indifference of the English people. The greatness of Spencer's reputation throughout the world was indeed scarcely appreciated in England. His name was as well known in America, and carried even greater influence perhaps in that country than it did in England. In all the European countries he was eagerly read ; even in Russia his works were studied by every social student of advanced thought.

Although Spencer's Philosophy won many disciples in every country of the world, it cannot be said that he founded any individual school of philosophy. And the reason is not far to seek. Spencer's philosophy is animated from beginning to end by a contempt of authority, by a championing of individual views, by a tendency to emphasise the importance of reasoning for oneself : all of which are in complete opposition to the spirit of discipleship. Spencer himself never was or could have been a disciple of anyone ; his whole constitution rebelled against it ; and it may be said that the same trait characterises those who are most imbued with the Spencerian spirit. They, too, are not cut out for discipleship : like Spencer himself, they are far more ready to criticise than to follow a master. Spencer teaches us to follow reason always and authority never : the philosophy of Spencerism precludes discipleship by its very nature. Thus, although even at the present day we find numerous individuals who profess themselves as ardent disciples, we usually discover that they have only an imperfect acquaintance with his works, and have missed the true spirit in which he wrote. And thus, notwithstanding all the criticism passed upon him in the course of the present work, I may claim without paradox to be a better Spencerian than they : I may claim, moreover, to represent the views which he would have certainly held for the most part had he flourished in the present century. We may be Spencerians either in spirit or in letter ; but if we are dogmatic adherents of Spencer's words we are no true Spencerians at all : we have missed the spirit and the real greatness of his work. We must not claim for Spencer that sort of finality which is claimed by the followers of Comte and other philosophers. For the only result of so doing is to belittle his great position in the history of thought and to betray also our own inability to appreciate the true significance of his work.

If we are true Spencerians in spirit—if, that is to say, we are prepared to pass the doctrines even of Spencer himself through the fire of uncompromising criticism—then, and then only, can we attain the right to speak of him as one of the greatest and most powerful minds of the nineteenth century. If we can see his faults in detail, we can then appreciate his fundamental greatness. We can see that in the whole history of the world there never has been a philosopher so deeply imbued with the spirit of liberty and of reason. We cannot, indeed, maintain that his doctrine of liberty was always well applied, nor that his reasoning was always correct. But if we Spencerians have imbibed the true feelings of liberty and reason, we shall be the first and not the last, to criticise the dogmatic theories of Spencer. And we shall believe that there is still no finer introduction to the sciences of biology, of psychology, of sociology, and of ethics than is to be found in Spencer's monumental works on these subjects. We know that *most* of his original theories are well founded ; but we wish to celebrate his name not by his words, but by his memorable battles for liberty and for reason, his impetus to the progress and refinement of civilisation. If, therefore, the reader has been inclined to cavil at the numerous criticisms of Spencer made in the present work, let him remember that *that* is the true Spencerian spirit, to which any acquiescence in authority is repugnant—even though it be the authority of Spencer himself.

We have seen in the course of this work that Spencer's life was wholly bound up in his philosophical convictions and principles. We need not raise any suggestion of egoism or *amour-propre* to explain the extreme unhappiness entailed upon him by the general deliquescence of his doctrines. When to that misfortune we add the wretched nervous condition into which he had fallen, we can well understand the almost hopeless misery in which his latter years were spent. He regarded himself as a man who had sacrificed money and health and life for what he conceived to be the public welfare. And this was his reward! Can we be surprised if, at the end of his Autobiography, he uttered a note of warning to those who contemplated a literary career? " Unless his means are such as enable him not only to live for a long time without returns, but to bear the losses which his books entail on him, he will soon be brought to a stand and subjected to heavy penalties." But " If the prompting motive is the high one of doing something to benefit mankind, and if there is readiness to bear losses and privations and perhaps ridicule in pursuit of this end, no discouragement is to be uttered; further than that there may be required greater patience and self-sacrifice than will prove practicable. If, on the other hand, the main element in the ambition is the desire to achieve a name, the probability of disappointment may still be placed in bar of it." . . . " Even should it happen that, means and patience having sufficed, the goal is at length reached and applause gained, there will come nothing like the delights hoped for. Of literary distinction, as of so many other things which men pursue, it may be truly said that the game is not worth the candle. When compared with the amount of labour gone through, the disturbances of health borne, the denial of many gratifications otherwise attainable, and the long years of waiting, the satisfaction which final recognition gives proves to be relatively trivial.

As contrasted with the aggregate of preceding pains, the achieved pleasure is insignificant. A transitory emotion of joy may be produced by the first marks of success ; but after a time the continuance of success excites no emotion which rises above the ordinary level."

Readers of the present work will perhaps already have discovered reasons for the belief that, if, Spencer was over-estimated in the nineteenth, he is certainly under-estimated in the twentieth century. He was plainly a product of his age. Figs do not grow from thistles, nor grapes from thorns. The great men of any age are the expression of the spirit of that age. In every era there are numerous men who possess the potentiality of becoming great if the environment is favourable to them. And each age brings out the peculiar type of men who most adequately represent it. The others remain dormant, or fill minor spheres. If John Bright had lived in our times, he would scarcely have been a distinguished politician ; he would probably not have been a politician at all. The age represents certain tendencies : the individuals who hold those ideals with the greatest conviction and urge them with the greatest force come to the fore. The rest drift into other lines of interest. So, too, Spencer was a pure Victorian —a " Maker of the Nineteenth Century." He flourished while his ideals were in fashion ; he withered when they passed away. But if we wish to estimate his real greatness, apart from the adventitious fluctuations of his environment, we shall inquire, not what was thought of him at different times, but what he did. We shall find that, without money, without special education, without health, he produced eighteen large volumes of philosophy and science of many diverse kinds ; that he invented an entire new system of philosophy which for half a century filled the attention of all thinking people ; that he led the chief controversies on Evolution and Biology without ever having received any tuition in those subjects ; that he wrote perhaps the most important text-book of Psychology of his century, without any acquaintance with the works of his predecessors, and scarcely any with those of his contemporaries ; that he established the science of Sociology in England ; that in all branches of so-called Moral Science he was recognised as a leader ; that he became the philosophic exponent of nineteenth century Liberalism ; that he published a variety of mechanical inventions ; and that on endless other subjects, great and small, he set forth a profusion of new and original ideas. A stable judgment will recognise in these achievements a true greatness, that may withstand all passing gusts of popular opinion.

BIBLIOGRAPHY

I.—LIST OF THE WORKS OF HERBERT SPENCER.[1]

A.

THE SYNTHETIC PHILOSOPHY.

" First Principles," 1862. 6th Edition, 1900.

" The Principles of Biology " : vol. i., 1864; vol. ii., 1867. Revised and enlarged edition, vol. i., 1898 ; vol. ii., 1899.

" The Principles of Psychology " : 1 vol., 1855. 2nd edition, vol. i., 1870 ; vol. ii., 1872. 4th edition, 1899.

" The Principles of Sociology " : vol. i., 1876. 3rd edition, 1885 ; part iv., " Ceremonial Institutions," 1879 ; part v., " Political Institutions, 1882 (parts iv. and v. were subsequently bound together to form vol. ii. of " The Principles of Sociology," 1882) ; part vi., " Ecclesiastical Institutions," 1885 (part vi. was subsequently bound up with two further divisions to form vol. iii. of " The Principles of Sociology," 1896).

" The Principles of Ethics " : part i., " The Data of Ethics," 1879 (part i. was afterwards bound up with two more divisions to form vol. i. of " The Principles of Ethics," 1892) ; part iv., " Justice," 1891 (part iv. was afterwards bound up with two further divisions to form vol. ii. of " The Principles of Ethics," 1893).

---

[1] All published by Messrs. Williams and Norgate, in London, and by Messrs. Appleton in New York.

B.

Miscellaneous Works.

" Social Statics," 1850 : àbridged and revised edition (bound up with " The Man *versus* the State "), 1892.

" Essays " : 1st series, 1857 ; 2nd series, 1863 ; 3rd series, 1874. American reprints of the first two series. Final edition (in three volumes), 1891.

" Education," 1861 (frequently reprinted) : cheap reprint, 1878.

" The Study of Sociology " (" International Scientific Series "), 1873 : library edition, 1880.

" The Man *versus* the State," 1884 : 2nd edition (bound with " Social Statics "), 1892.

" The Nature and Reality of Religion," 1885 (suppressed).

" Various Fragments," 1897 : enlarged edition, 1900. One of these " fragments," entitled " Against the Metric System " (1896), was re-issued separately in 1904 with additions, under a provision in Spencer's will.

" Facts and Comments," 1902.

" Autobiography," 1904.

Spencer re-issued his father's " Inventional Geometry " with a preface in 1892 ; and he published a " System of Lucid Shorthand " by his father in 1893.

C.

Descriptive Sociology.

No. 1, *English*, 1873.

No. 2, *Ancient Mexicans, Central Americans, Chibchas, and Ancient Peruvians*, 1874.

No. 3, *Types of Lowest Races, Negritto Races, and Malayo-Polynesian Races*, 1874.

No. 4, *African Races*, 1875.

No. 5, *Asiatic Races*, 1876.

No. 6, *American Races*, 1878.

No. 7, *Hebrews and Phœnicians*, 1880.

No. 8, *French*, 1881.

Since Spencer's death, the following further instalments have been issued :—

No. 9, *Chinese*, 1910.

No. 10, *Greeks : Hellenic Era*, 1910.

(The series is still in progress.)

II.—LIST OF WORKS DEALING WITH HERBERT SPENCER.[1]

Of these there are something over one hundred ; the great majority of little value. The following are the most important :—

Allen. "Personal Reminiscences." By Grant Allen. Published in the *Forum* for April-June. New York, 1904.

Duncan. "Life and Letters of Herbert Spencer." By David Duncan, 1908.

Edinburgh Review. Art. "Herbert Spencer," July, 1908.

Hudson. "A Character Study of Herbert Spencer. By W. H. Hudson. Published in the *Fortnightly Review*, January, 1904. "An Introduction to the Philosophy of Herbert Spencer" (containing a biographical sketch). By W. H. Hudson, 1895, 1897, 1904. "Herbert Spencer." By W. H. Hudson. 1908.

Macpherson. "Herbert Spencer, the Man and His Work." By Hector Macpherson. 1900.

Royce. "Herbert Spencer." By Josiah Royce, with a chapter of personal reminiscences by James Collier. New York, 1904.

Thomson. "Herbert Spencer." By J. Arthur Thomson. 1906.

Werner. "Herbert Spencer." By Edward T. C. Werner. Shanghai : Kelly and Walsh, Ltd. 1913.

[1] All published in London, except where otherwise stated.

Among other works which throw light upon Spencer or his Philosophy the following are the best known :—

Beare. "Organic Morality; or, Ethics of Herbert Spencer." By J. I. Beare. Dublin, 1889.

Collins. "Epitome of the Synthetic Philosophy." By F. Howard Collins. 5th edition. 1901.

Fiske. "Outlines of Cosmic Philosophy." By J. Fiske. 1874.

Gaupp. "Herbert Spencer." By Otto L. Gaupp (Stuttgart). 1897.

Gingell. "Aphorisms from the Writings of Herbert Spencer." By Miss J. R. Gingell. 1894.

Grosse. "Spencer's Lehre von der Unerkennbaren" (Leipzig). 1890.

Huxley. "Life and Letters of T. H. Huxley." By Leonard Huxley. 1900.

James. "Memories and Studies." By William James. 1911.

Mackay. "A Plea for Liberty." With an Introduction by Herbert Spencer. Edited by Thomas Mackay. 1891.

Mikhailovsky. "Qu'est-ce que le Progrès ? examen des idées de M. Herbert Spencer." By N. K. Mikhailovsky. Paris, 1897.

Roberty. "Comte et Spencer." By E. de Roberty. Paris, 1894.

Sidgwick. "Lectures on the Ethics of T. H. Green, Mr. Herbert Spencer, and J. Martineau." By Henry Sidgwick. 1902. "Lectures on the Philosophy of Kant, and other Lectures and Essays." By Henry Sidgwick. 1905.

Sorley. "The Ethics of Naturalism." By W. R. Sorley. 1904.

Under an endowment an annual lecture is delivered at Oxford University in memory of Herbert Spencer, and bearing the title " Herbert Spencer Lectureship." Few of them have any connection with Spencer's work, except very indirectly. The lecturers have been as follows :—

1905. Frederic Harrison.
1906. Hon. Auberon Herbert.
1907. Francis Galton.
1908. Benjamin Kidd.
1909. Professor G. C. Bourne.
1910. Raphael Meldola, F.R.S.
1911. William Bateson, F.R.S.
1912. Professor D'Arcy Thompson.
1913. C. Lloyd Morgan, F.R.S.
1914. Hon. Bertrand Russell, F.R.S.
    (All these have been published at Oxford.)
1915. J. M. Baldwin.

CHRONOLOGICAL TABLE

1820. Birth of Spencer.— James Mill's "Essay on Government."

1822. Birth of Pasteur.

1825. Birth of Huxley.

1826. First Railway opened between Stockton and Darlington.

1827. Birth of Lister.

1832. Reform Bill passed.

1833. Spencer went to live with his uncle near Bath.

1836. Spencer's first article, "Crystallization," in the *Bath and West of England Magazine*.

1837. Accession of Queen Victoria.—Spencer started life as a schoolmaster.— Began engineering under Charles Fox.

1838. First publication of " Bradshaw's Guide."—Spencer appointed to *Birmingham and Gloucester Railway*. — English Chartists published "The Charter."

1841. Spencer left the *Birmingham and Gloucester Railway*.

1842. Letters to the *Nonconformist* on " The Proper Sphere of Government."

1843. Publication of J. S. Mill's Logic.

1844. Graham's Factory Act in England. — Spencer appointed sub-editor of the *Pilot*.—Returned to engineering.—Birth of Nietzsche.

1845. Height of railway mania.

1846. Repeal of the Corn Laws.

1846–9. Final repeal of Navigation Acts.

1847. Factory Bill passed.

1848. Revolution in France.—Macaulay's History of England, vol. i. — J. S. Mill's "Political Economy." — Spencer appointed sub-editor of the *Economist*.

1850. Spencer made the acquaintance of G. H. Lewes.

1851. Spencer's first book, "Social Statics."—Spencer met George Eliot and introduced her to Lewes.

1852. Publication in the *Leader* of Spencer's article "The Development Hypothesis," advocating a theory of Evolution.—Spencer made the acquaintance of Huxley.

1853. Gladstone's first Budget.—Spencer resigned post on the *Economist*.

1854. Crimean War began.—Breakdown of Spencer's health.

1856. Treaty of Paris.

1857. Spencer's article on "Progress: Its Law and Cause," foreshadowing the doctrines of "First Principles."—Indian Mutiny.—Death of Comte.

1859. Darwin's "Origin of Species" published.—Rise of Volunteer movement in England.

1860. Spencer published the programme of, and began to write, his System of Philosophy.—Death of Schopenhauer.

1861. Outbreak of American Civil War.

1862. "First Principles."

1864. Foundation of the *x* Club.

1865. Death of Cobden.

1866. Death of Spencer's father.—Atlantic Cable successfully laid.—Spencer joined the Jamaica Committee.—Reform Bill defeated.

1867. Lister's first publication on the Antiseptic System.—Disraeli's Reform Bill passed.

1868. Abolition of Church rates.

1869. Irish Disestablishment carried.

1870. Elementary Education Act.—Franco-Prussian War.

1873. Foundation of the journal *Mind.*—Death of John Stuart Mill.

1875. Final Establishment of the French Republic.

1877. War between Russia and Turkey.

1878. Death of G. H. Lewes.

1879. Spencer's visit to Egypt.

1880. Death of George Eliot.

1881. Battle of Majuba Hill.

1882. Foundation of the Anti-Aggression League.—Spencer's visit to America.

1883-4. Nietzsche's " Also Sprach Zarathustra."

1893. Matabele War.—Death of Tyndall.

1895. Spencer declines the German Order " Pour le Mérite."—Death of Huxley.—Death of Pasteur.—Röntgen discovered X-rays.

1896. Completion of the Synthetic Philosophy.

1898. Spencer went to live at 5, Percival Terrace, Brighton.

1899. Outbreak of the Boer War.

1900. Death of Nietzsche.

1902. End of the Boer War.

1903. Death of Spencer.

INDEX